Praise for Brenda M

For *Season of the Body*:

Her work in the creative nonfiction genre allows her to combine body memory with intellectual memory, creating personal essays that reflect one woman's spiritual and cultural experience. . . . The resulting essays are memorable for their sensuality and unflinching honesty.

—*Library Journal*

In this collection of affecting and thought-provoking essays, Miller . . . addresses how so many people try to move determinedly forward in their lives, but often find themselves "doubling back" and "playing out the same plots again and again." Likewise, the forward motion of each of these essays tends to loop back and revisit themes of love, loss, loneliness and healing. —*Publishers Weekly*

Season of the Body is the graceful accumulation of a patient soul and an attentive eye. Brenda Miller has created an elegant collection of essays born out of blood, bone, and flesh. Her language is organic and sensual: the kind of authentic prose that can only be crafted out of an authentic life. This is a book of great beauty by a writer whose work meets the world at a critical time when we are praying for illumination. Brenda Miller's voice is a beacon of light.

—Terry Tempest Williams, author of *Refuge:
An Unnatural History of Family and Place*

For *Blessing of the Animals*:

Brenda Miller writes with such extraordinary grace and intimacy that, despite our weariness and fears, we find ourselves falling in love with the world all over again.

—Kim Barnes, author of *In the Wilderness: Coming of Age
in Unknown Country* and *A Country Called Home*

In *Blessing of the Animals*, a new dog leads Brenda Miller to explore the blurred edges between the physical and the spiritual, to probe the connective tissues of magnetism, memory, and mysticism. Contemplating the process of aging and the dilemmas of desire, she seamlessly fashions an aesthetics in which the human body can be solidly aware of the moment even as it is soaring "on the verge of flight."

—Judith Kitchen, author of *Distance & Direction*

Delicate, elegant, and occasionally devastating, Brenda Miller's essays are helping to set the standard for our generation.

—John D'Agata, author of *Halls of Fame*

Listening Against the Stone

SELECTED ESSAYS

Brenda Miller

Skinner House Books

Boston

Printed in the United States

Cover painting by Odilon Redon, *La Cellule d'Or* (1892), photograph © The Trustees of the British Museum/Art Resource, NY. Used by permission.
Cover design by Kathryn Sky-Peck
Author photo by Phil Rose Photography
Text design by Jeff Miller

print ISBN: 978-1-55896-643-7
eBook ISBN: 978-1-55896-644-4

6 5 4 3 2 1
13 12 11

Library of Congress Cataloging-in-Publication Data

Miller, Brenda, 1959–
    Listening against the stone : selected essays / Brenda Miller.
        p. cm.
    ISBN 978-1-55896-643-7 (pbk. : alk. paper) — ISBN 978-1-55896-644-4 (ebook)
        1. Miller, Brenda, 1959– 2. Spiritual biography—United States. I. Title.
    BL73.M55A3 2011
    200.92—dc22
    [B]

                                                        2011015593

Essays were previously published as follows:

Brenda Miller, *Blessing of the Animals* (Eastern Washington University Press, 2009): "Blessing of the Animals," "Raging Waters," "Enticement," "Opalescent," "Secret Machine," "A Different Person," previous version of "Incantations" ("Runes and Incantations")

Seattle Weekly: "The 23rd Adagio"; *Shenandoah*: "Hungers"; *Mindful.org*: "Dirty Windows"; *Another Chicago Magazine*: "Music of the Spheres"; *Superstition Review*: "I Need a Miracle"; *The Sun*: "The Burden of Bearing Fruit"; *Sweet: A Literary Confection*: "Our Daily Toast."

Brenda Miller, *Season of the Body* (Sarabande Books, 2002): "Next Year in Jerusalem," "How to Meditate," "Basha Leah," "A Thousand Buddhas," and "Infant Ward." Reprinted with the permission of The Permissions Company, Inc. on behalf of Sarabande Books, www.sarabandebooks.org.

The author also gratefully acknowledges permission to use the following copyrighted materials: Lyrics to Grateful Dead songs ("I Need a Miracle" and "Althea"), © Ice Nine Publishing Company, used with permission; William Stafford, excerpt from "Choosing a Dog" from *The Way It Is: New and Selected Poems*, copyright © 1998 by the Estate of William Stafford, reprinted with the permission of The Permissions Company, Inc. on behalf of Graywolf Press, Minneapolis, Minnesota, www.graywolf press.org; "Galileo" from *Light's Ladder* by Christopher Howell, reprinted with the permission of the author; "The Ghost Trio" from *The Ghost Trio* by Linda Bierds, reprinted with the permission of the author.

Sometimes from sorrow, for no reason,
you sing.

—WILLIAM STAFFORD

Contents

AT THE EDGE OF THE WORLD

Acknowledgments

My deepest thanks to all the organizations that support my writing: The Helen Riaboff Whiteley Center, where a majority of these essays were written; Cottages at Hedgebrook; the Virginia Center for the Creative Arts, the Ucross Foundation; and Washington State Artist Trust.

This book would not be possible without the love, guidance, and companionship of many people: Lee Gulyas, Suzanne Paola, Bruce Beasley, Holly Hughes, Nancy Canyon, Katie Humes, Sheila Bender, Joel Long, Robert and Cheri Van Wagoner, Kimberly Peters, Vicki Hsueh, the women of Booklift, and all my students and colleagues at Western Washington University and the Rainier Writers Workshop.

Preface

I recently attended a rehearsal for the Threshold Choir—a group of women who sing at the bedsides of those who are terminally ill or dying. The choir rehearses every other week in the parlor of a funeral home, and the members invite anyone to join them, regardless of singing ability. Since I was a child, I've always been told I was tone deaf, and I usually only mouth the words at sing-alongs, but lately I've felt an openness to my voice when chanting *Om* in yoga class; even my reckless harmonizing in the car on the way to work seems to hit the right note sometimes. I thought maybe it really wouldn't be so hard.

The choir sings simple songs, with repeating refrains that let the mouth open wide in round vowels, each individual voice merging with the whole. In the center of the funeral parlor they set up a patio recliner, the kind that supports you from every angle so it feels like you're floating, and for one song I sat in that chair while the choir toned around me, voices blending on a single note. And I felt something—like small hands on my knees, my ankles, my neck. I felt the voices resonate in my own chest. I wanted, then, to be able to sing, *really* sing: to carry someone like that with my voice.

But, as the choir director put it tactfully during intermission, I have "a little difficulty sustaining the tune." I probably won't be back, but for those few hours I still sang. Quietly. Listening more than singing, hearing how a voice, if you let it, might find the right level on its own. I knew then the gift this singing brings to someone facing death, but I also heard it as a balm for the living—a way to acknowledge our collective loneliness, our vulnerability, and to make these things not only bearable but fertile ground for joy.

I'm a writer, not a singer, but I would like to believe that writing can mimic this kind of song. And as I experienced in the Threshold Choir, to sing well, you must *listen* well. You listen to the voices around you, and you hear how your own voice rises in response. In all my work, I want to listen more than speak: listen with my ear pressed against the stone of holy places, the posture of all supplicants.

In this book, I'm bringing together selections from my work that form a picture of how my sense of spirituality has evolved and shifted through the years: constantly changing, but always rooted in a strong desire for connection. Together, these essays develop the story of a single woman making her way, stumbling but always seeking out allies—a dog, a friend, a painting, a tree—to help her gain her true bearings. Sometimes I turn to oracles, and sometimes I turn to prayer; sometimes just a meal with good friends, or a walk with the dog, spurs gentle epiphanies.

In the first section, "Blessings," I trace my growth as a young girl raised in a conservative Jewish household to a woman who eventually travels as a reluctant tourist to Israel and lays her head against the stones of the Wailing Wall, trying to find there the necessary guidance to pray. I follow a circuitous path that leads to a Unitarian church, my dog in my arms, as I acknowledge all the different blessings—human and animal—that have been bestowed in my life. In the second section, "A Thousand Buddhas," the essays focus on the way Buddhist meditation and a devotion to yoga become more essential to my efforts at finding stillness and balance, and these practices also teach me how precarious such balance can be. Finally, in the third section, "At the Edge of the World," I find myself turning to arts of all kind to help me articulate a life where all the hard emotions dwell hand in hand with happiness.

Throughout it all, I'm singing my heart out: maybe off key, sometimes in harmony, and often with just a hum that takes over my body. Then I grow quiet and simply listen. When we listen like this, in the aftermath of song, we surrender ourselves to exactly what *is*—a faint smile on our lips for a moment or two as the melody fades away.

BLESSINGS

Incantations

I've always believed in signs, and will do almost anything to predict the future. Often the first to pry open my fortune amid the remains of a Chinese dinner, I inhale the smell of the cookie itself as prophecy: that honeyed shellac, the faintest bitter whiff of lemon. I like best those moments just *before* my future will be revealed, the cookie still whole in my hands, my fate untouched within its folds. When the time comes, I read the fortune aloud with scorn, I laugh with my dinner companions, I add the words "in bed" to every line because that's what's done these days. But secretly I believe anything the fortunes say; I stash these ribbons away in my purse where I'll come across them weeks, months, years later and won't be able to remember if what they said came true.

This predilection for the mystic has been with me ever since I was a child. The best present I ever received as a girl was the Magic 8 Ball: every day I asked it a question, my hands sweaty on the black orb; then I turned it over so the answer floated up with sharp clarity from the murk: *It depends, No, All signs point to yes*. I found such limited and simple answers liberating rather than confining; I suppose I felt comforted by the possibilities whittled down to a certain few, the future determined in the simplest words possible. Even if the answer disappointed I resisted asking the question again, wary of contra-diction. Once answered, forever answered: that's what I believed. I could hop on my bike—the pink Schwinn with its white wicker basket—and pedal up the cul-de-sac to carry out whatever course of action the 8 Ball dictated, whether it be the wisdom of playing hide-and-seek with the Steinberg kids (notorious cheaters, every one), or asking for a swim in the Goldman's pool (the most lovely blue water, the most suggestive mermaid shape), or dropping my best friend Stacy because she had spread my current infatuation with Bill French all over the fifth grade.

Perhaps this constant truck with the Magic 8 Ball makes me seem an anxious child, chronically indecisive, raised in a household where punishment might be meted out for the smallest misstep. Nothing could be farther from the truth. My parents were mild people, given to rare outbursts of anger but on the whole thoroughly predictable: my father drank the same glass of Ovaltine every morning; I knew where to find my mother at any time of the day. They drank exactly one glass of Manishevitz wine on the holidays, and three days out of seven we ate Jell-O chocolate pudding for dessert, mounded with tantalizing swirls in fancy glass cups. My future—my day-to-day fu-ture anyway—was never in question: I knew my father would always have a job (he worked as a mid-level engineer for RCA and later, with ITT; he retired after forty years and said all he missed was his daily bridge game at lunch). I knew my mother would come home from the market every Thursday with bags and bags of food for us to plunder (soft rye bread with caraway seeds, boxes of Hostess cup-cakes, Cocoa Krispies: food well-known, well-loved). I knew I would get up from my bed, every weekday for years, and walk to school: first the elementary school a couple of blocks away, then Patrick Henry Junior High, a little farther, then Granada Hills High School, across the busy intersection. The eucalyptus trees would continually shed their bark but never disappear. The 7-11 would always have root-beer Slurpees and I would have the money in my pocket to buy them.

I had the same friends year in and year out: Valentina (whose name was much too exotic for her tastes; she forced us to call her Tina, but secretly I whispered *Valentina* to myself like a love-sick incantation); Jana, with her electric red hair; Stacy, with her white-carpeted living room we could never touch. My mother did her best to ensure no part of my life might hold unpleasant surprises, and we always performed practice runs for any new undertaking. For instance, she drove with me on the route I would walk to my summer school, and even mimed the stop I would make at Jana's house, silently beeping the horn, pretending to call out, as practice, for my friend to join me.

Perhaps it was this very predictability that made the occult so alluring. It's an odd paradox, as I think of it now: this keen desire to believe some kind of unknowable (and uncontrollable) current ran beneath the placid surface of day-to-day life, and at the same time, wanting desperately to pin this crazy current down, make it, well, *predictable*.

In this, I think I was no different than the majority of my compatriots; all of us rushed home after school to tune our old black-and white televisions to *Dark Shadows*. We followed with cult-like intensity the doings of Barnabas Collins and his ilk as they terrorized the mortal Victoria and the rest of Collinwood for a half-hour each day. We followed along those shadowy stairways, rattled the doors of secret rooms. We held elaborate debriefing sessions in the backyard—post-*Dark Shadows*, pre-dinner—in that twilight when nothing-to-do takes on the exact rhythm of a swing, the mournful creak of the teeter-totter.

Dark Shadows arrived in our lives during the same era as *Twilight Zone* and *Outer Limits*; these shows came on at night, after dinner, and this fact, in itself, imparted more significance: we watched these programs not with our friends but with our families, in the safe hearth glow of our televisions after the sun had set. Homework had been done. Baths taken. Our parents sat on the couch behind us, smoking and flicking their cigarettes into ashtrays deep as soup bowls; we lay prone on the floor, legs scissoring the air above us.

We all kept inventory of our favorite episodes and loved intoning, in perfect Rod Serling imitation, *You are about to enter another dimension, a dimension not only of sight and sound but of mind. . . .* But the only episode I can recall now, years later, was called "Little Girl Lost." In it, a six-year-old girl finds herself—accidentally of course—wandering around in another dimension. This dimension existed right behind her living room wall; she fell in, but couldn't get out. You could hear her, you could even see a bulge now and then in the plaster. Her father ends up diving in after her—slithering through the wall and grabbing her arm to return the girl to her three-dimensional existence.

When we weren't arousing our occult senses through TV, I went along with my friends, heart pounding, into their darkened bathrooms to "do the Bloody Mary." Being Jewish, I didn't realize, at the time, the profound religious implications of this ceremony. We closed the door of the bathroom, lit one candle, and placed it next to a mirror. Then, joining hands, we chanted "I Believe in Bloody Mary, I Believe in Bloody Mary" over and over, our little voices moving from the sonorous range of the monk into the squeal range of the deliciously frightened. We said it faster and faster, the force of our voices supposedly calling forth a vision of the Virgin Mary, bloodied (I surmise) from her encounter with her crucified son. We were supposed to keep our gazes fixed on the mirror, where the candlelight magnified every shadow and caught every glimmer, but at some point my eyes closed of their own accord, squeezed tight, until finally one of us screamed "I see her!" and we could then tumble out of the bathroom, gasping and laughing, "Oh my god, oh my god, I saw her, did you see her?" We all shrieked *yes!*, before making our intoxicated way through the hall and back into the bedroom of the perpetrator (needless to say, we could only perform this particular ritual with the mother of the house safely preoccupied elsewhere; I doubt any mother of this era looked kindly on a game that involved fire, satanic chanting, and the possible soiling of her good towels).

I now have grave doubts that any of us really saw the Bloody Mary—surely someone finally screamed just to end it all—but still I have in my mind a vision of that dark angel, hovering in the corner of a bathroom mirror, her arms outstretched, blood dripping down her robes. In the mirror, I can see soap in a dish shaped like a clamshell, the fake tulips in a plastic vase, the air freshener on a shelf above the toilet, the toilet paper neatly hung with one square folded back—all the ordered contents of a suburban bathroom safely cupboarded—and in that one high corner, the floating Mary, eyes cast down, hands bloody, beseeching our help.

Now I'm sure I could find someone eager to tell me how this archetype taps into a young woman's fear of menstruation, but at the time I knew we had somehow, through our incantation, at least nudged that membrane between worlds, bulging into heretofore unknown dimensions. I walked home after these encounters, and the white sidewalk seemed to pulse out an unearthly light, the ivy-covered slopes of neighboring yards glistened an unreal green. Whether I interpreted this altered state of consciousness as fright or ecstasy, I really can't say; I suspect it was a muddled combination, the buffer between the two spheres thinner than I'd ever imagined.

At slumber parties we often held impromptu séances, not so much to contact the dead, but to see if we could levitate—physically levitate—ourselves out of our earthly domain. I always secretly longed to be the chosen candidate, and one fortuitous evening, I was. I lay down on the floor in the center of the circle of young girls; I'm sure Tina must have been there, in all her regality (that long white neck, the sharp pointed nose), and Jana (looking particularly "witchy" with her wild red hair). Again, we darkened the room and lit a candle. Each girl slid two fingers of each hand under my body, so that I felt my friends at every directional point—at my head, my feet, my arms, my hips—like spokes in a wheel. Their touch felt both light and firm on my body—a touch I would recognize years later in massage school, that same vibrant attention in the fingertips, that same spark—and I almost relaxed into their hands until they started to chant. "Light as a feather . . . ," they intoned, "stiff as a board . . . Light as a feather . . . stiff as a board . . . ."

I had chanted this myself many times, as part of the outer circle, and I knew what was expected of me. This mantra was designed to contact powers from above, our dead ancestors, who would make me into the prototype of a corpse: stiff with rigor mortis, then weightless to make the ascent to heaven. My friends would lift me with their fingertips, and let go to see if I might hover in midair. If so, it meant the dead had smiled on us, that the mild bedroom in which we played had been converted into a portal to the spirit world.

The incantation continued, sonorous, growing louder, perhaps a little impatient, and I heard one girl (Tina?) sigh. Someone darted her hand out from under me to wipe her nose then put her fingers back, slightly more moist than before. The candlelight flickered across the ceiling, picking up the sparkly glitter of the stucco. I closed my eyes and tried to let the voices enter me and resonate through my bones. Whether from the power of a suggestion, or fear, or the strong desire to please, I *did* feel the muscles contract along the full length of my body until I had acquired the requisite plank-like quality. "Light as a feather . . . stiff as a board. . . ." I let the voices wash into me, hollow me out. The girl at my head and the girl at my feet somehow signaled to one another and they all began to lift, the pressure of their small fingerpads holding me in a circumference of concentration and care, the likes of which I wouldn't know again until years later, transported by the light but relentless caress of a lover's hands.

And now I felt it, I felt myself ascending an inch off the ground, and higher. The chanting grew fractured with nervous giggles, and "oh my god's" and before I knew it they had all pulled their hands away and I fell, with a decided thump, back to earth. The girls rolled out of the circle shrieking and holding their sides, the noise of which brought a stern reprimand from the voice of a parent up above.

I'm sure I rolled on the floor with my friends, too, laughing and gasping for breath. But I would like to imagine that somehow our spell worked, for just a few seconds longer. I would like to remember myself suspended, the voice of incantation wrapping me in a light reverberant and new. I want to be that figure you see suspended in a painting—a soul in the moment it has left the body, placid and calm, not yet frightened at the long journey it must make alone.

As a child, I probed beneath the sunny surface of my life to intuit darker, more interesting forces at work; years later, as a teenager, I essentially performed the opposite task: puzzled by a life that seemed

increasingly dark, painful, and full of unpleasant surprises, I wanted
to find a current of lightness, or perhaps proof of a philanthropic
sentinel, like the good witch of the north. I wanted her to provide,
in the most chipper way possible, a clearly defined path to follow
(and if it happened to be paved in gold, so much the better).

Tina and Jana were now gone, off to colleges far away; my new
circle of friends, for some reason, consisted mostly of men, all of them
childhood buddies from their own neighborhood across the San Fernando Valley. I met Jonathan first, in a Reader's Theater program at
my first year of college in the suburban university just down the street
from my parents' house. At the peak of my Reader's Theater career,
we traveled together to Irvine for a competition where I won honor-
able mention for my earnest rendition of Sylvia Plath's "Lady Laza-
rus." I remember standing on the stage in a frightful red dress, teeth
bared and arms aflutter as I attempted to raise myself from the dead.

My first boyfriend, Kevin, and I took a class together called
"Ethnobotany of Hallucinogenic Plants." That classroom held an
odd assortment of earnest biology majors, with their taxonomic flash
cards, and people like Kevin and me: suburban hippies, dressed in
overalls and tie-dyed shirts, our faces bright with expectation. I think
we hoped for a kind of "how-to" cooking class, and while we found it
interesting that Mayan shamans drank their own urine after ingest-
ing Peyote buttons, we couldn't figure out a way to put this new
knowledge into practical application.

All of us sat for hours on the high, flat rocks off Mulholland
Drive, staring off into the star-filled sky, the glow of cannabis or the
slight prismatic effect of mushroom tea forming a connective and
protective aura around us. We listened to Crosby, Stills, Nash, and
Young; or Bob Dylan; or Genesis or Heart and took the lyrics as a
kind of anthem: "There's something happening here," we'd lip synch,

"what it is ain't *exactly* clear. . . ." The air, those nights, seethed with light—so clear it was easy to maintain the illusion we existed on the lip of the world, far from suburbs and sophomore year of college and jobs in the student bookstore. We were somehow . . . *bigger* than all that, so large this world could barely contain us.

I loved my boyfriend, Kevin, with the kind of clarity and forgiveness that comes only with first loves: that terrain of romance still so fresh, the paths not yet trampled, the fences not yet forged. Our lovemaking had the quality of communion: our bodies nearly transparent, merging like ghosts wandering lost from other worlds. When he looked at me in just the right way, I could believe that separation is only an illusion, that if we perceive the world rightly it will reveal its multiple dimensions to us all at once. And not just romantic love accomplished this feat, but platonic love as well: In my circle of friends, the presence of these men, I felt the way I had as a young girl, in the center of the séance, lifted by hands that could surmount any force that conspired to keep me down.

Years after Kevin and I split up, my friend A.J. gave me a deck of Tarot cards. My friends and I had studied Tarot for years—intrigued by the vivid symbolism, the resonant images, the way these images kindle one's intuition. I'd quickly learned that this ancient tool of divination, refined after centuries of use, requires patience, a respect toward the cards, a willingness to sift through the myriad possibilities to arrive at an answer. I still wanted clear-cut resolutions—a simple *unlikely*, or even the couched but hopeful *all signs point to yes*—but I knew even then that such resolutions are temporary at best, that any answer we might encounter is continually primed for revision.

A.J. and I had taken a hike high into the mountains above Lake Tahoe; that night, at our cabin, A.J. read the Tarot cards for me. His deck, an unusual one, called on images from Mayan culture: minions rowing canoes, cages of parrots, gods on their thrones. Their costumes seethed with gold and silver, fiery reds and cool turquoise blues. The gods wore leopardskin capes and held their hands up in signs of benediction.

A.J. began to lay out the cards in the traditional Celtic Cross formation: ten cards, each placement representing domains of past, present, and future. I'd be lying to say I understood, then, all the intriccies of Tarot nomenclature or even remember what question I asked for guidance, but one card in particular has stayed in mind all these years: Temperance. In this card, a young person acts as intermediary between sky and earth: light pours into the tree at her side, light pours out of a cup she tilts toward a pond. One foot touches the water; one foot touches the ground. She is a mere channel for these natural forces, her body transparent as gauze.

A.J. lit a Marlboro and gazed at the cards a long time. He tapped one finger on Temperance. The colors blazed at me: sky blues, lake blues, forest greens, the delicate light of the sun. "What do you see here?" he asked.

I wanted to say "balance, poise," the obvious traits the card revealed. But instead no words came. I felt tears starting, but they merely rose to the surface and hovered there. While Temperance, I could see, was quite beautiful, she also seemed quite lonely: a young woman struggling on her own to hold everything in balance at once. I knew any kind of poise I might feel was a veneer, masking the vast store of anxiety that defined my true self. I only held my life together, I wanted to tell A.J., through the presence of my friends: those boys who surrounded me and made me feel beautiful, wild, untamed. I had yet to understand, the way I could in later years, the meaning of the word "Temperance"—how clarity can overtake a person when she reins in a little the broad sweep of her passion.

I remained silent, and A.J. nodded, as if we had come to some wordless agreement about my future. He moved on in the reading, pointing out the Death card and the Fool (both cards would recur with annoying frequency throughout my life). When he was done, we kept the cards on the table a long time, a pattern of lovely images that shifted and changed under our gaze.

Later that night, when A.J. handed me the Mayan deck and told me it was mine, I didn't really believe him. Here was an object he knew intimately, loved deeply, and he simply handed it over, wrapped in black silk. He had once told me that Tarot cards must be a gift if they are to hold their true power; it just didn't work to buy them yourself. I've since learned this is not the case, but I still like the impulse behind this particular myth: that in order for an oracle to provide, it needs as backup the generous favor of a friend. "They speak to you," A.J. said, and that was enough.

After I left L.A. I used this Tarot deck for years, consulting my *Tarot for Beginners* book, but the interpretations my friends devised rang more true: the cards acted as a divine Rorschach test, reflecting back desires too hidden for ready articulation in more customary ways. Even if I'd known these people only a few hours, they often laid out queries of the most personal nature: should I get pregnant now? should I leave my husband? As we looked at the cards—my fingertip tapping the Queen of Pentacles, say, or drawing attention to the mirror that both unites and divides the Lovers—we drew closer together, our shoulders touching.

I ended up living for several years at a communal hot springs resort in northern California. At Orr Hot Springs, I bathed every day in the mineral water, steamed myself in the sauna, jumped into the cold-water pool and swam a long time while my mind drifted and cleared. Such days felt oracular, the dimensions of my life multiplied tenfold: I could hear the river and I could smell the jasmine; I could see naked bathers coming and going from the bathhouse. I anticipated every move a half-second before it occurred: the turning of a book's page by a reader on the lawn, the opening of the sauna door, the exact splash of a swimmer in the pool.

My companions and I often sat at kitchen tables in the evening, after a good meal and wine, and either did Tarot card readings for each other or consulted the I-Ching. For the I-Ching, an ancient oracle that spoke in cryptic phrases we had to decode in order to make a decision, I used three pennies, the shiniest ones I could fish from my pocket, instead of traditional yarrow sticks. I asked a question, threw the coins, and constructed the Chinese hexagrams from the way the coins fell, heads up or down. Some configurations involved "changing lines," and I duly noted all these in my I-Ching workbook, showing how one glyph changed into another and the actions I should take to make my future sound.

One of the last times I seriously consulted the I-Ching, I was by myself in a little hotel on the coast, in the town of Albion. The time had come for me to buy a share in Orr Hot Springs, to become a bona-fide paying member of that community or move on. I was 26 years old. The smell of that rented room stays with me: the salt of the Pacific, the damp wallpaper, coffee in the kitchen down below. Alone, and feeling lonely, for the first time in years, I got out my pennies and held them in my fist a while, warming them before writing out the question: "What would be the effect of committing to Orr Springs?" I threw the pennies; they clattered down. The lines accrued and what I got, of course, was the I-Ching equivalent of "it depends."

Perhaps I sat and stared at the pennies a while, or, more likely, I got up and gazed sadly out the window to the gray horizon and the calligraphic lines of the surf down below. The tide, I could tell, was on the way in, and I knew all night I'd be kept awake by the pounding of the waves on the beach below my room. But in the morning the ocean would have retreated to lick placidly at the pinnacled rocks off shores. The I-Ching, literally translated, means "The Book of Changes," and I wanted so much to believe in the book's fundamental premise: that change cannot be avoided and so one must gracefully surrender.

I knew it was time for me to leave Orr Springs, but how would I survive, I thought, without those hot waters, without that particular circle of friends to sustain me? I felt, at that moment, a little like the girl in *Twilight Zone* who falls into another dimension: neither here nor there but somewhere in between, a little blurred around the edges. She waits, alone, for the hand of someone she loves to claim her.

Now, years later, I'm sustained by so many things; my home, my dog, my grown-up friends who are so willing to laugh and commiserate over the most mundane concerns. But I often feel as though I've become dense—too solid to really let anything mysterious penetrate, much less transport me beyond the measure of my own skin. I look at the palms of my hands and try to read there some clue to the future, but the lines do not seem portentous, merely deep wrinkles that speak of ordinary, everyday change.

I once had a student who typed fragments of her story on little strips of paper and slipped them inside homemade fortune cookies. She passed around a basket of these treats and asked us to break into them. We gleefully did so, snapping the cookies apart and pulling out the strips of "fortune." It was up to us to put the story together, as a group, by chance and circumstance. And I'm starting to believe, truly, that all our stories might be enacted this way: the bits and pieces of life floating around at random until our friends help arrange them into sense.

Sometimes on Wednesday nights, when I'm with my sangha—my community of Buddhist friends—we perform a sutra service and sing "The Heart of the Prajnaparamita," or the "The Threefold Vow of Refuge." When it's my turn to be bellmaster, I start the chants hesitantly, never sure if I'm on key, but soon enough my compatriots join in, and their voices do not obliterate but amplify the sound of my own. In the vow of refuge we chant, "I take refuge in the Buddha, I take refuge in the Dharma, I take refuge in the Sangha." It's the sangha, the circle of friends that closes the prayer on a three-part downbeat that resonates for a long time. As we chant together, my mouth opens wide and these lovely vowels emerge: breath distilled to incantation, strong enough to straddle dimensions, seductive enough to coax anyone back from where she may have wandered alone.

Basha Leah

You are here to kneel
Where prayer has been valid.

— T.S. ELIOT

I

In Portugal I walk slowly, like the old Portuguese men: hands crossed behind my back, head tilted forward, lips moving soundlessly around a few simple words. This posture comes naturally in a country wedded to patience, where the bark of the cork oak takes seven years to mature, and olives swell imperceptibly within their leaves. Food simmers a long time—kid stew, bread soup, roast lamb. Celtic dolmens rise slab-layered in fields hazy with lupine and poppies.

It's very late. I've drunk a lot of wine. I don't sense the cords that keep my body synchronized, only the sockets of my shoulders, my fingers hooked on my wrist, the many bones of my feet articulating each step. I'm flimsy as a walking skeleton; a strong breeze might scatter me through the eucalyptus.

A few days ago, in a sixteenth-century church in Évora, I entered the "Chapel of the Bones." Skulls and ribs and femurs mortared the walls, the bones of five thousand monks arranged in tangled, over-lapping tiers. A yellow lightbulb burned in the dank ceiling. Two mummified corpses flanked the altar. A placard above the lintel read: *Nos ossos que aqui estamos, Pelos vossos esperamos.* "We bones here are waiting for yours. . . ." Visitors murmured all around me, but not in prayer; none of us knelt in front of that dark shrine. What kind of prayer, I wondered, does a person say in the presence of so many bod-ies, jumbled into mosaic, with no prospect of an orderly resurrection? A prayer of terror, I imagined, or an exclamation of baffled apology.

II

On Shabbat, the observant Jew is given an extra soul, a *Neshama Yeterah* that descends from the tree of life. This ancillary soul enables a person to "celebrate with great joy, and even to eat more than he is capable of during the week." The Shabbat candles represent this spirit, and the woman of the house draws the flame toward her eyes three times to absorb the light.

In California, one rarely heard about such things. We grilled cheeseburgers on the barbecue, and bought thinly sliced ham at the deli, ate bacon with our eggs before going to Hebrew school. Occasionally we visited my grandparents in New York; they lived in a Brooklyn brownstone, descendants of Russian immigrants, and they murmured to each other in Yiddish in their tiny kitchen. They reflexively touched the mezuzah as they came and went from their house. When I watched my grandmother cooking knishes or stuffed cabbage, I imagined her in *babushka* and shawl, bending over the sacred flames while her husband and daughters gazed at her in admi-ration. So I assumed my mother must have, at some time, lit the

Shabbat candles and waited for the *Neshama Yeterah* to flutter into her body like a white, flapping bird.

But when I ask my mother about this, she says no, she never did light the candles. "I didn't really understand," she says. "I thought the candles were lit only in memory of your parents, after they died." She remembers her mother performed a private ceremony at the kitchen counter every Friday evening, but didn't call for her daughters to join in the prayers. My grandfather worked nights, as a typesetter; he might have worked on Shabbat, doing whatever was necessary to feed his family in Brooklyn during the Depression, and so my grandmother stood there alone, in her apron, practicing those gestures that took just a few moments: the rasp of the match, the kindle of the wick, the sweep of the arms. She did this after the chicken had roasted, the potatoes had boiled, and the cooking flames were extinguished. But my mother, this American girl with red lips and cropped hair, was never tutored in the physical acts of this womanly ritual.

The *Neshama Yeterah* departs with great commotion on Saturday night. To revive from the Shabbat visitation, a person must sniff a bouquet of spices "meant to comfort and stimulate the ordinary, weekday soul which remains." The ordinary, weekday soul? Does he pace through the arteries and lungs, hands behind his back, finding fault with the liver, the imperfect workings of the heart? "Some cinnamon is all I get?" he mutters. "Some cloves?" In my family, the word *soul* was rarely mentioned, but my mother, and my grandmother, chanted the Jewish hymn, "eat, eat," as if they knew our ordinary, everyday souls were always hungry. As if they knew we had within us these little mouths constantly open, sharp beaks ravenous for chicken liver and brisket, *latkes* and pickles and rolls.

III

Outside the spa town of Luso, in the Buçaco woods, in a monastery built by the Carmelite Monks, the shrine to Mary's breast flickers inside a tiny room. I open the cork door, sidle in sideways, and face a portrait of the sorrowful Mary who holds her naked breast between outstretched fingers, one drop of milk lingering on her nipple. The baby Jesus lies faceless in her arms, almost outside the frame, the lines of focus drawn to the exposed breast and the milk about to be spilled. Hundreds of wax breasts burn on a high table, and tucked among these candles are hundreds of children—faded Polaroids of infants in diapers, formal portraits of children with slicked back hair, stiff ruffles, and bow ties. The children's eyes, moist in the candle-light, peer out from among the breasts and the bowls of silver coins.

The tour guide describes the shrine in Portuguese, using his hands to make the universal symbol for breast. I catch the word *leite*; of course the milk is worshipped here, not the breast itself, that soft chalice of pleasure and duty. I want to ask: what are the words of the prayer? Is the prayer a prophylactic or a cure? But my language here is halting and ridiculous. Whispers linger in the alcove, *Por favor, Maria, Obrigada, Por favor.*

I want to kindle the wick on Mary's breast, but I don't know the proper way—how much money to drop in the bowl, or the posture and volume of prayer.

At home, in Seattle, I volunteer once a week on the infant's ward at Children's Hospital. I hold babies for three hours, and during that time become nothing but a pair of arms, a beating heart, a core of heat. I'm not mindful of any prayer rising in me as we rock, only a wordless, off-key hum. Most of these children eat through a tube slid gently under the skin on the backs of their hands; pacifiers lie gummy on their small pillows as they sleep. I'm sure there's a chapel in the hospital where candles stutter, and a font of holy water drawn from the tap and blessed. Maybe a crucifix, but more likely secular stained glass illuminated by a wan bulb. Mary's breast will not be displayed, of course—the distance between these two places is measured in more than miles—but the succor of Mary's milk might be sought nonetheless.

It will be quiet. The quiet is what's necessary, I suppose, and an opportunity to face the direction where God might reside. I imagine there are always a few people in the chapel, their lips moving in various languages of prayer, including the tongue of grief.

IV

Our synagogue was near the freeway in Van Nuys, California, and it looked like a single-story elementary school, with several cluttered bulletin boards, heavy plate-glass doors, gray carpet thin as felt. White candles flickered in the temple; the Torah was sheathed in purple velvet; gold tassels dangled from the pointed rollers. Black letters, glossy and smooth as scars, rose from the surface of the violet mantle. When the rabbi, or a bar-mitzvah boy, brought the Torah through the congregation, cradling it in his arms, I kissed my fingers and darted out my hand to touch it, like the rest of the women.

In Hebrew school, we learned the greatest sin was to worship a false idol. "God is not a person," my teacher said, "but God is everywhere." The Torah, though we respected it, was not God. The alphabet, though it was a powerful tool, was not God. Abraham and Isaac and Moses were great men, not God. "God is everywhere," my teacher said. "Like the air." I learned about Exodus. I learned about

Noah's ark. I learned about the Burning Bush. These miracles were played out by faceless figures smoothed onto the felt-board. The twenty-two letters of the alphabet paraded like amiable cartoons across the top of the classroom wall, and I was called by my Hebrew name—*Basha Leah*, which over time was shortened to *Batya*. I preferred the elegance of *Basha Leah*, enfolded by lacy veils, while *Batya* turned me into a lumpy dullard, dressed in burlap, switching after the mules.

In the temple, the drone of the prayers rose in a voice close to anger from the men, nearer to anguish from the women, then ebbed into a muttered garble of tongues. I tried not to look too hard at the rabbi, lest I should worship him. I averted my eyes from the face of the cantor. I ended up staring at my feet, squished and aching in their snub-nosed shoes. My mother's hand fell like a feathery apology on the back of my neck, and I swayed uncomfortably in place. The ache in my feet rose through my body until it reached my eye sockets.

"I've had it to up here," my mother sometimes cried, her hand chopping the air like a salute at eye level, grief and frustration rising in her visible as water. In the synagogue, waters of boredom lapped through my body, pouring into every cavity, like a chase scene from *Get Smart*. I imagined my soul as a miniature Max, scrambling away, climbing hand over hand up my spine to perch on the occipital ridge until the waters began to recede.

V

There's another kind of soul that enters the body—a *dybbuk*, "one who cleaves." A *dybbuk* speaks in tongues, commits slander, possibly murder, using the body of a weak person as a convenient vehicle. If roused and defeated, this soul will drain out through the person's little toe.

The word *dybbuk* is in me, part of my innate vocabulary, though I don't know how. Perhaps from the murmured conversations of my relatives in Brooklyn and their neighbors, the women with the billowing housedresses and the fleshy upper arms. I was only an occasional visitor to these boroughs saturated with odors of mothballs and boiled chicken, soot and melted snow. I may have heard the Yiddish words in the exchanges between my paternal grandmother and the customers in her knitting shop; I blended into a wall of yarn, camouflaged by the many shades of brown, in a trance of boredom, as the women clustered near the cash register. "That one's a *golem*," they might say, nodding in the direction of a simple-minded man in the street. A *golem* meaning a zombie, a creature shaped from soil into human form, animated by the name of God slipped under the tongue. Or, "He's possessed of a *dybbuk*," they might whisper of a neighbor's child gone bad. They gossiped about *nebiches* and *schlemiels*, the bumbling fools who never quite got anything right, swindled from their money or parted from their families through ignorance or bad luck.

Sometimes I sat next to my grandfather after he woke in the afternoons, and he explained the transformation of hot lead into letters, the letters into words, the words into stories. I held my name, printed upside down and backwards on a strip of heavy metal. My grandmothers pinched my cheek and called me *bubbele*—little grandmother. They cried "God Forbid!" to ward off any harm. On Passover I opened the front door and hollered for Elijah to come in; I watched the wineglass shake as the angel touched his lips to the Manishevitz. I closed my eyes in front of the Hanukkah candles and prayed, fervently, for roller skates.

VI

In the central chapel of the Carmelite monastery in the Buçaco woods, dusty porcelain saints enact their deaths inside scratched glass cases. Above each case the haloed saint, calm and benedictory, gazes down on the lurid scene below: a small single bed, a man's legs twisting the bedclothes, his thin arms reaching out in desperation. The witnesses (a doctor called in the middle of the night? A maid, nauseated by the bloody cough of her master? A scribe, summoned to write the last words?) recoil from the bed in a scattered arc.

And the saint? Somehow he's beamed up and transformed into the overhanging portrait, the eyes half-closed, the halo pressing into place the immaculately combed hair. One finger touches his lips as if to hush the tormented figure below. His arms have flesh; the lips are moist; the background is lush and green.

We have our heaven, too, though I don't remember the mention of Paradise at Temple Ner Tamid. Paradise, I thought, was for the Gentiles; when my Christian friends asked me if I would go to heaven, I sorrowfully shook my head no. They looked at each other, and then at me, touching my shoulder in sweet-natured commiseration. "We don't believe in Jesus," I said, my voice trailing off. I thought our religion was about food. It was about study, hard work, persecution, and grief. But I've since learned there is a Paradise for the Jews; it is, in fact, the Garden of Eden, where the Tree of Life grows dead center. "So huge is this tree that it would take five hundred years to pass from one side of its trunk to the other." We even have a hell: *Gehinnom*, where "malicious gossip is punished by hanging from one's tongue, and Balaam, who enticed the Israelites into sexual immorality, spends his time immersed in boiling semen." Of course, such things weren't mentioned when I was a child.

But my mother covered the mirrors with black cloth when her father died. She sat in mourning, with her mother, for seven days. She may have even spoken the Kaddish for twelve months, since my grandfather had no sons. Certainly she lit the Kaddish candle on Yom Kippur. But I was a child. I didn't listen, or I didn't understand, that the soul remains attached to the dead body for seven days, and takes twelve arduous months—ascending upward, flopping downward, cleaning itself in a river of fire—to enter Paradise. I didn't realize the soul needs our help, in the form of many and repeated prayers.

Before me now, a saint is dying in his rectangular case, on a narrow bed covered with a single woolen blanket. I surreptitiously cross myself, the way I've seen people do. The gesture, so delicate, touching the directional points of my body—my head, my heart, my two arms—seems far removed from the passion of Christ. It doesn't feel like a crucifix I inscribe on my body, but the points of a geometrically perfect circle. I curl one fist inside the other, and I kiss my knuckles, I bow my head. I don't know if I'm praying. It feels more like I'm talking to myself.

VII

Swaying in prayer is "a reflection of the flickering light of the Jewish soul . . . or it provides much-needed exercise for scholars who spend most of their day sitting and studying." I get out my yoga mat; I sway down into a forward bend and stay there a long time, breathing, and then roll up, one vertebra on top of the other until I stand perfectly straight, aligned. I think about moving a little, and I do, like the oracle's pendulum that swings to and fro in answer to an unspoken question.

VIII

When I was sixteen, I became president of my Jewish youth group, and we set out to create *meaningful* Shabbat ceremonies, feeding each other *challah* on Friday night, reading passages from Rod McKuen, holding hands in a circle and rapping about our relationships. We petitioned for and received permission for a slumber party, properly chaperoned by our counselors—college students in their early twenties. The minutes from the planning meetings illustrate our real concerns: "It was decided no one under the age of twenty can sleep on the couches." "Challah will be split equally before anyone begins to eat." "Ronnie says no wine. So Mike's in charge of the grape juice." We rented spin-art machines. We got a ping-pong table. We decided to give Ronnie a bar-mitzvah.

Ronnie had a black mustache and dreamy brown eyes. He wore tight jeans and read Dylan Thomas. When he confessed that he'd never been bar-mitzvahed, we clucked over him like a gaggle of grandmothers. We made plans in the bathroom. We took out every prayer book we could find. We found him a yarmulke and a dingy tallis to drape across his shoulders. *"Baruch Atah Adonai,"* we chanted in unison, *"elohanu, melach ha'olum. . . ."* We closed our eyes, and the prayers trailed off when we didn't know the words; we moved our lips in the parched, desperate way of the old people in synagogue. We swayed back and forth; we felt mature, and very wise. Someone gave a speech enumerating all of Ronnie's strong points. Ronnie gave a speech telling us how he expected to improve in the coming years. We improvised a Torah with pillows, and we made him walk among us, beneath an arch made of our intertwined hands.

I think he cried then, his lips scrunched tight together, a Kleenex in his hand. I remember his thanks, and I remember us sitting in a circle around him, our eager hands damp with sweat, our satisfied faces aglow.

IX

I call home from a post office in Lisbon. My booth, number four, is hot and dusty, my hands already clumsy with sweat, and I dial the many numbers I need to connect me with home. Like the Kabbalists, manipulating the letters of the alphabet, I work this dreary magic. Travel has not agreed with me. I have a fever, and I want to lie down, but my pension has a dark, steep staircase and soggy newspapers in the windows holding back the rain.

My mother answers the phone. I picture her at the kitchen counter: the long wall of photographs tacked together on a bulletin board—all the children, my two brothers and I, peering out at my mother from our many ages. She sits in the green vinyl chair, reflexively picking up her ballpoint to doodle. The lace *Shalom* hangs motionless in the entry. A red-clay Menorah sits on the mantel, the candleholders shaped like chubby monks, their hands uplifted.

"How's everything?" I ask. We talk in a rush. "How are *you?*" she asks again and again. Not until I'm almost ready to hang up does she mention: "Well there is a little problem."

"What?"

"Everything's a little *meshuga,*" she says, and her voice gets that catch; I can see her biting her lower lip, pushing her hand up into the hair at her forehead. "I'll put your father on," she says, and I hear the phone change hands.

"Your mother," he says.

"What?"

"Your mother had to have a hysterectomy. They found some cancer."

"What?"

"She's okay," my father says. "Everything's okay."

"A hysterectomy?"

"They got it all, the cancer. They found it early enough. Don't worry."

I'm breaking out in a damp sweat across my face, under my arms. I can't think of anything to say but, "Why didn't she tell me herself?"

"Don't worry," my father says. "Everything's fine."

I decide to believe him. After a few more distance-filled exchanges, our voices overlapping with the delay, I hang up. I push my way past the people waiting for my booth, I pay my *escudos*, I walk out on the Avenida Da Liberdade among the taxis and the buses. I start walking to the north, but I don't know where I'm going, so I turn around and head to the south along the busy, tree-lined boulevard. I stumble past the National Theater, past a vendor selling brass doorknockers the shape of a hand. What am I looking for? A synagogue? Or another shrine, this one to Mary's womb?

"In the womb a candle burns," the Kaballah tells us, "the light of which enables the embryo to see from one end of the world to the other. One of the angels teaches it the Torah, but just before birth the angel touches the embryo on the top lip, so it forgets all it has learnt, hence the cleavage on a person's upper lip."

I want to light a candle, the flame sputtering in a bed of salt water and blood. If I had the lace scarf my grandmother gave me when she died, I might slip into a stone synagogue, cover my head, and follow the words of the Torah. But I don't know how. I don't know to whom I'd be praying; I thought we weren't allowed to worship a human

God, so I eradicated the concept of God entirely. *It was all a mistake,* I want to say now. *I wasn't listening.* I don't know how to take the alphabet and assemble the letters into a prayer.

There is a Kaballah tale about an illiterate man who merely uttered the Hebrew alphabet, trusting that God would turn the letters into the necessary words. His prayers, the story goes, were quite potent. But I can hardly remember the alphabet. *Alef, Gimmel, Chai. . . .* I don't remember the Hebrew word for "please." I remember the words *Aba, Ima.* Father, Mother. I remember the letters tripping across the ceiling, the letters minus their vowels, invisible sounds we needed to learn by heart.

X

A touch of the angel's finger, and knowledge ceases. I touch my lip, the cleavage. *Do you remember?* I ask myself. *Do you?* Something glimmers, like a stone worn an odd color under the stream, but my vision is clouded by a froth of rushing water. Perhaps knowledge exists in the amnion; the fluid is knowledge itself, and the angel's fingernail is sharp; his touch splits the sac, and drains us dumb.

The *mikveh* is a gathering of living waters—pure water from rain or a natural spring. This public bath was the center of any Jewish village; the water refined the body, washed off any unclean souls residing there. A woman stepping into these baths purified herself before marital relations with her husband; on emergence the first object she spied determined the kind of child she might conceive. If she saw a horse, this meant a happy child. A bird might equal spiritual beauty. If she saw an inauspicious omen—a dog, say, with its ugly tongue, or a swine—she could return to the bath and start again.

"The Talmud tells how Rabbi Yochanan, a Palestinian sage of handsome appearance, used to sit at the entrance to the *mikveh*, so that women would see him and have beautiful children like him. To those who questioned his behavior, he answered that he was not troubled by unchaste thoughts on seeing the women emerge, for to him they were like white swans."

What do I see when I step from my tub? My own body, lean and young in the mirror, kneeling to pull the plug and scrub the white porcelain. What do I see when I step from the baths of the Luso spa? Water arcing from the fountain, and all the Portuguese women gathered round its many spouts: bending forward, kneeling, holding out cups and jugs to be filled. A grandmother—in black scarf, wool skirt, and thick stockings—turns to me and smiles.

XI

At my cousin Murray's house, brisket and matzoh balls and potato kugel lie heavy on the oak table. The curtains were drawn; I think of them as black, but they couldn't have been. They were probably maroon, and faintly ribbed like corduroy. I remember an easy chair; and my cousin in the easy chair looking too tense to be reclined; he should have been ramrod straight, the murmur of relatives lapping against him. My memory is hazy with the self-centered fog of childhood, the deep boredom, my eyes at table height, scanning the food.

"If only she'd gotten the dog," someone murmured, not to anyone in particular. This must have been a funeral. I remember my cousin Anita being "found." I didn't understand what that meant, but my cousins were sitting in the living room, covering their faces with their hands. Their yarmulkes slipped sideways off the crowns of their head. I remember the gesture, that's all—three grown men, slumped in chairs, their hands covering their eyes as if they couldn't bear to see any longer. As if they had already seen too much.

I don't think I went to the service. All I remember clearly is the food on the table: platters of chicken, congealing; baskets of knotted rolls; tureens of yellowish soup. And the men in the living room, so contorted in their grief. When I think of my cousins, I see them framed between the legs of adults, in a triangle of light, frozen. No one ate. All that food: for the extra souls, the one extra soul who wouldn't leave the room, even though the burial must have taken place according to Jewish Law, as soon as possible. Someone must have washed the body, anointed her with oil, wrapped her in a shroud. But a soul hovered in the corner of the room, a darkness smudging the corners of my vision. Eat, someone said, it is good to eat, and a plate was brought into my hands.

XII

"One who cleaves." The definition of the word "cleave" is two-fold and contradictory: to cleave means both to split apart and to adhere. Perhaps one is not possible without the other. Perhaps we need to break open before anything can enter us. Or maybe we have to split apart that to which we cling fast.

In yoga class, my teacher tells us to "move from the inner body." We glide our arms and our legs through a substance "thicker than air, like deep water." We swim through the postures. The Sphinx pose. Sun Salute. Tree. I generate intent before the muscles follow. I breathe deeply, I stretch sideways, I reach up, I bring my hands to-gether at my heart. *Namasté*, I whisper. *Namasté*. I know my access to composure is through attention to the pathways and cavities of my body, so I sit cross-legged, my forehead bent to the ground in a posture of deep humility. Sometimes, then, I feel whatever *dybbuks* cling inside me loosen their hold; they begin the long slide down my skeleton to drain out through my little toe.

XIII

I have a snapshot taken of me when I was eighteen. I've got long straight hair, and I'm wearing a Saint Christopher medal around my neck. It falls between my breasts. On another, shorter chain, I wear a gold "chai," the Hebrew letter for "life." It clings to the bare skin between my collarbones.

The medal was given to me by my first boyfriend—a boy I cleaved to, a boy by whom I was cleaved, split apart. I was *crazy* for him. I wanted the medal because I had seen it on his chest; I had gripped it in my fingers as we made love. He draped the pendant over my head, and kissed me between the eyes.

Eighteen years later, I still have Saint Christopher—a gnarled old man carrying a child on his shoulder, a knotted staff clutched in one hand. He dangles off the edge of my windowsill, next to a *yad* amulet inset with a stone from the Dead Sea. I have candles on the windowsill, their flames swaying to and fro, like little people in prayer.

A Catholic friend tells me that Saint Christopher is no longer a saint; the Vatican has declared him a nonentity. His life is now a mere fable about the Christ child crossing a river on the ferryman's shoulders, growing so heavy he became the weight of every bird and tree and animal, the combined tonnage of human suffering. But the ferryman, being a good man, kept at his task, his knees buckling, his back breaking, until he had safely ferried the small child to shore. "It's just a story," my friend says, but I don't understand how this tale differs from the other Biblical accounts: the walking on water, the bread into body, the wine into blood. "It is different," my friend assures me. "Saint Christopher never existed."

But I know people still pray to him. They believe he intervenes in emergency landings, rough storms at sea, close calls on the freeway. Words of terror and belief form a presence too strong to be revoked. I still take him on the road; *it couldn't hurt,* as my grandmother used to say, with that small Jewish shrug, an arch of her plucked eyebrows. All this, whatever you call it—superstition, religion, mysticism—do what makes you happy, *bubbele.*

XIV

Alef, Gimmel, Chai. . . . I recite the letters I know, and they grow steady as an incantation, a continual flame. The Kabbalists manipulated the letters into the bodies of living animals and men. They know an alphabet behind the alphabet, a whisper that travels up the Tree of Life like water.

White swans. I dream I am wrapped only in a white sheet, and the Chasidic men turn their square shoulders against me; they will not touch me, they will not talk to me, because I am a woman. I am unclean and dangerous. If I do not follow the law—if I do not light the Sabbath lamp, if I touch the parchment of the Torah, if I look at a man while I'm menstruating—I will be punished by death in childbirth. Punished when I'm most vulnerable, during the act that makes me most a woman. But what about Miriam? I plead. What about Rachel, and Leah, and Ruth? They were women. They saved us. It is a woman who brings the Sabbath light into the home. It is a woman who resides as a divine spirit in the Wailing Wall. But the men, in their black coats, their black hats—the men turn away. They ignore me. I grip the white sheet tighter against me as the men file into the synagogue, muttering.

XV

I'm staying in a pink mansion on a hill overlooking Luso. It used to be the residence of a countess, and the breakfast waitress makes fun of my halting Portuguese. *"Pequeno Leite,"* I say in my submissive voice as she raises the pot of warm milk. I only want a little, but she drenches my coffee anyway, laughing.

In the evening I stroll down a winding street, past two women waiting at their windows, their wrinkled elbows resting on the sill. I don't know what they're waiting for: children to come home, or perhaps the pork to grow tender in the stew. They wave to me, amused. Another woman splashes bleach outside her doorway and kneels to scrub the already whitened stone. Bougainvillea, bright as blood, clings to her windowsill. Men are nowhere in sight; this appears to be a province maintained entirely by women. I make my way to a stone bridge and watch the sun sink beyond fields of flowering potatoes.

In the distance, women harvest vegetables in a field. I think they are women, but I can't be sure; all I see are the silhouettes of their bodies bending, and lifting, and bending again. These women—are they the ones who walk to the monastery and tuck pictures of their children between Mary's breasts? Do they pray before that altar? I don't know; they seem always to be working, or resting from their work.

Back in the square, the Portuguese men emerge to sit in clusters, wearing hats and wool vests; they walk down the lanes, their hands behind their backs, or they stand together, leaning on wooden canes. I sit on a bench facing the fountain, and the men converse around me, all inflection and vowels, grunts and assents. I'm silent as a hub, turned by words without meaning, without sense.

XVI

The *luz* bone is a hub, unyielding. "An indestructible bone, shaped like an almond, at the base of the spine, around which a new body will be formed at the Resurrection of the Dead." The *luz* bone feeds only off the *melaveh malkah*, the meal eaten on Saturday night to break the Sabbath. It's a bone without sin, taking no part in Adam's gluttony in the garden; so, our new bodies on the day of judgment will be sweet and pure.

For proof of its durability, three men in a Jewish village tested a *luz* bone. (Like magpies, did they pluck the bone out of the rubble of an old man? or of a woman dead in childbirth? or of a child?) They smuggled the Luz bone to the outskirts of their village, to a black-smith's shop, the fires glowing red in the stove. They thrust the ver-tebra in the coals; they plunged it under water; they beat upon it with sledgehammers. I can see them, these men dressed in ripe wool, sweating, their black hats tilted back on their heads. They hold it up to the light of the moon, the bone glossy from its trials, but intact. It's smooth as an egg, oval and warm.

XVII

"Those who bow to God in prayer are thought to guarantee them-selves a resurrected body, because they stimulate the *luz* bone when they bend their spine."

Downward-Facing Dog: the sit-bones lifted upward. Forward bend. Triangle. Warrior I, II, III. Sphinx. Cobra. Cow. These words come to me like directives, and my body twists and bends and turns, gyrating in a circle around the *luz* bone.

The Tree. I balance on one foot, the other pressed into my thigh. I put my hands together in front of my chest. I breathe. I look past my reflection in the window; I focus my gaze on the trunk of a holly. I grow steady and invisible. The alphabet hangs from my branches like oddly-shaped fruit.

Child's pose. I curl into a fetal position on the mat.

Nu? I hear my mother's voice across a great distance. *Nu, bubbele?* She pats one hand on her swollen abdomen, and holds it there. I want to answer, but from my mouth comes a watery language no one can understand.

Next Year in Jerusalem

Why is this night different from all other nights?

At Passover every year, I dipped the greens in salt water to remind me of my ancestors' tears, and I chewed on parsley to remind me life is bitter, and I raised my glass of grape juice and hollered "Next year in Jerusalem!," clinking my glass hard against my cousin Murray's. At Passover, no matter how much I've grown, I remain a clumsy girl in chiffon dress and opaque tights, sitting at the children's table, my stomach growling as my little brother asks a question. His voice is halting but already proud of the story for which he's responsible. I look at him with envy while I suck grape juice off of my fingers.

Why tonight do we eat only matzoh?

My cousin Murray, a small man but imposing in his navy blue suit and graying beard, refers us to our texts, the *Haggadah* that tells us the answers to these questions, but I've stopped listening. We dip our pinkies in red wine and fingerprint the ten plagues onto the rim of our plates. What are they? Locusts swarming the fields, hail made of fire, days of total darkness, rivers turning to blood. Ho hum. I eye the roast egg, the *haroses*, the matzoh on the Seder plate. It's always dark in my cousin's house; what light there is seems reflected off the gold-foil inlay on the Passover dishes. My cousins smell of Brut and horseradish. I eye the roasted shank of a lamb, its blood the mark of the Chosen Ones. I watch Elijah's cup. I wait for the touch of the prophet's lips.

Why tonight do we eat bitter herbs?

The Seder goes on and on; the voices around me rinsed of meaning or sense. I chew on matzoh and *haroses*, imagining slaves' hands slapping mortar between the bricks, the heavy poles biting into their shoulders as they draw cartloads full of the stuff to the pyramids. Someone is talking about the Red Sea, and I think of Yul Brynner chasing the Hebrews in his chariot, leather straps around his biceps, his bare chest glistening. I think of Charlton Heston at the edge of a cliff, the frightened Hebrews clustered around his robes. The walls of the sea part, and the Chosen Ones gallop through, wild-eyed in fear and wonderment.

Why tonight do we dip them twice in salt water?

As I grew older, my grape juice changed to Manishevitz wine, and I murmured the prayers dutifully with the rest of my family. When I was twelve, my parents gave me a choice: I could spend another year in Hebrew School and get bat-mitzvahed, or quit Hebrew school right away. Our school was a stuffy classroom annexed to the synagogue, with tiny desks and battered chalkboards. For three hours each Saturday, I sat in that room and chanted the Hebrew alphabet, recited Hebrew phrases such as "Mother is making the bread," and heard the tired stories of Abraham and Isaac, Noah and his nameless wife, Moses and the golden calf.

Of course, I chose to quit the place, my freedom those mornings as miraculous to me as that of the slaves in the Sinai. But my brothers, being boys, underwent the coming-of-age ritual, and they received bags of *gelt*, gift certificates, trips to New York. They held the Torah cradled in their arms, paraded it through the aisles of the synagogue while we kissed our fingers to touch the velvet mantle.

After my brothers were officially men, the Passover Seder grew shorter and shorter—the four questions reduced to one, the matzoh on the table lying almost untouched as we snuck into the kitchen for bread and butter.

From Hebrew school I had a detailed picture of the old Jerusalem in mind: the stone walls, the arched gateways, biblical light streaming into rooms where wondrous and miraculous things happened. I imagined black-suited scholars hurrying toward the *yeshiva*, though I'd only seen such men from a distance, during my family's occasional visits back to the sooty neighborhoods of Brooklyn and Queens.

I left home and forgot about Passover most years, until the care package arrived from my mother: an orange box of egg matzoh, a sleeve of dry *mandelbrot*, a can of macaroons so sweet they made my teeth ache. I'd forgotten, I thought, those words spoken so many times during my childhood.

Next year in Jerusalem!

The clink of the wine glasses. The open door for Elijah. The *afikomen* in its white cloth hidden somewhere behind the Encyclopedia

Britannica. We watched *Yentl* and *Fiddler on the Roof*, the tinny klezmer music a soundtrack to our lives as Jews in America.

No one in my family had ever been to Israel. No one really wanted to go. We had reached our own Promised Land: the warm, enclosed cul-de-sacs of the San Fernando Valley, where we lived in our tract house with a Doughboy swimming pool in a spacious back yard. We lived among minor television stars (the "Jack" from the children's show *Jack in the Box*, the girl who teased Tony the Tiger on the Frosted Flakes commercial). We ate cheeseburgers from McDonald's, and brought home heavy, greasy boxes of chocolate chip Danish from the kosher bakery.

I traveled to Europe when I was eighteen, tramping through England, France, Germany, and Italy for three months; when I returned home, my grandfather asked me about my travels. His eyes gleamed as I told him stories about drinking espresso on the Left Bank of the River Seine, and eating peaches big as grapefruit on the coast of Italy. Finally he said, "And Israel? Tell me about Israel." He sat back and folded his hands expectantly across his chest.

I told him I hadn't gone. His smile vanished. He sat forward and dismissed me by focusing his watery gaze on the far wall of the living room where a *Shalom!* mosaic faced the main entry, and a *mezuzah* nestled in the doorframe.

"How could she be so close," my grandfather murmured, "and not visit the land of our people?"

I bit back my automatic protests; even then, I knew the physical distance between Italy and Israel was not the issue. The point was that a good Jewish girl would have bypassed Europe altogether—avoided the topography of the holocaust, and found her way to the Promised Land unimpeded.

Why is this night different from all other nights?

On July 2, 1994, I crossed the River Jordan into the West Bank. I crossed in a Jordanian bus full of Palestinians with American passports. My boyfriend Keith and I had our names written in Arabic on a permission slip from the Jordanian Department of the Interior. The river itself was a muddy trickle I could barely see; wild reeds grew thick in the mud of its banks. Though I was a non-religious Jew, I had still expected to feel *something* as I crossed into the Promised Land.

At the time, I did not think of myself as acting out a quest narrative archetypal for a Jewish woman. I did not recall the book of Exodus, recounted every year at Passover, my brother asking the four questions, the ten plagues, the angel of death, the parting of the Red Sea just a hundred miles to the south. I was afraid, as my ancestors must have been, but I was afraid of bombs and gunfire, not of Yul Brynner in his gaudy chariot. I was worried about the length of my dress, and the Syrian and Jordanian visas in my passport. Arafat had just visited Jericho for the first time in twenty-seven years, and the right-wing Jews in Jerusalem responded by breaking all the windows of the Arab-owned shops outside Damascus Gate.

My rayon dress clung to my damp thighs as an Israeli soldier boarded the bus. His hair was slicked back with mousse, and his khaki shirt hung open to the navel. He smelled, surprisingly, of Irish Spring. On his chest, a golden star of David swayed between his dog tags. "Passports!" he shouted, his voice cracking like an adolescent's.

I held mine out to him. He flipped through it, stopping on the page with the thick Syrian stamps. He looked at me, holding my passport just out of reach.

"How was Syria?" he asked.

Did he know I was Jewish? Did he expect a denunciation of the Arab countries, a declaration of fealty to Israel? Or was he flirting with me, just making small talk? The Palestinian woman in the window seat steadfastly looked the other way.

"Syria was great," I finally said, directing my words to his pendant.

He said nothing, but his lips curled up in what could be taken as a smile. He tossed my passport back into my lap and continued down the aisle of the bus. His rifle swung out as he turned, butting against my shoulder, leaving the tiniest of bruises.

In 1967, I had paraded through the schoolyard with my Jewish friends during the Six-Day War; we cheered Israel, our fists raised playfully in the air. Syria was the enemy—of Israel, of the United States, of the Jews. I confused the Syrians with the Nazis, all of them in uniform, with dogs, rounding up Jews as a preface to execution. When I heard the word "Syria"—with its sibilant "s," its insinuating lilt—I saw only three things: sand, barbed wire, and blood.

I was wrong, of course. Keith and I, in our wanderings through the Arab countries, had encountered nothing but hospitality and eager friendship. In Aleppo, Syria, the streets were lined with stalls selling green soap stacked like bricks, mounds of cardamom in open bins, amber jars of rose water and orange blossom oil. We drifted by vendors selling *schwarma*, with lamb roasting on giant spits. Men lounged in the doorways of their shops, sipping tea, or they tilted backward on straight-back chairs, rocking to the rhythm of the crowd. They waved and called to us, "Where from?"

We answered, hesitantly at first, "America," and the men cried, *Welcome!* They leapt to offer a chair, a spare tire, a piece of cardboard. "Please sit!" When we passed a baklava shop the owner frantically waved us in. We communicated with grins and a smattering of French. He gave us sweet pastry and fried eggplant and Cokes. His three young daughters popped inside, swirling around each other in pretty flowered dresses, their black hair bobbed short. They stopped when they saw us, eyes wary, but after conferring with their father they came to us and kissed our cheeks. Their lips were weightless as butterfly wings, and their eyes regarded me solemnly as I took each of their hands in mine.

It was a Friday, the holy day for the Muslims, and Keith and I went back into the streets, drawn by the staticky call of the *muezzin*. The women were dressed in their formal Friday attire—blinding white scarves edged with lace, jet-black robes, black gloves, not an inch of skin showing. Heat waves rose off the broken gray asphalt, a surface that turns to smooth marble as one approaches the Grand Mosque.

When we stepped into the courtyard, an old man angrily waved us into an antechamber. He plopped a heavy black robe over my shoulders, slapped up the hood on my head, demanded money from Keith, and shoved us out again. The black hood cut off my peripheral vision, so I teetered across the vast courtyard in a cocoon, my vision reduced to the patterns of white and gray tiles, squares within squares, leading to the central mosque.

Inside, thick Persian carpets cooled our feet, laid out in a tidy mosaic, greens flowing into reds into browns and maroon. Men and women crowded up against a grated window; they wiped the grate with their palms, then brushed themselves from head to toe, kissed their fingers, rocking back and forth in prayer. We inched inside the crowd and spied something the shape of a head, draped with a blue cloth. Prayers thrummed all around us.

"Welcome." A heavyset man with graying hair and a white mustache loomed over us, smiling. He shook our hands. "From where are you?" he asked. And then, waving one hand toward the pulpit, he smiled. "It is the head of Zachariah, the father of John the Baptist," he says. "A great prophet. Come, sit down."

Mehmet introduced us to his wife, a young woman with a face round as flatbread, hugging a curly-haired toddler to her hip. She smiled at us, but said nothing as we followed them outside, to a raised colonnade surrounding the courtyard. A commotion erupted by the eastern gate, and a wooden casket emerged high above a crowd, bobbing on its way toward the inner sanctum. Men in Western dress led the mob, running back and forth across the perimeter until the casket disappeared inside.

The minaret's loudspeaker emitted the soft buzzing that prefaces an imminent call to prayer. From across the courtyard, the bent figure of the gatekeeper rushed toward us.

"Can we stay?" Keith asked Mehmet.

"Yes, of course. You are my guests."

The old man, furious, pushed in close to Mehmet, who spoke back to him in a low, growling murmur. Both of them shot glances in my direction, and Mehmet returned to us, shaking his head.

"You may stay, but your wife," he said, pointing to me, "must go sit with the women."

Of course I would go; I didn't mean to offend. The gatekeeper waited, his arms folded, until he saw me stand up. Then he scurried away. I meandered along the edge of the courtyard, the wool cloak scratching my arms and the back of my neck, the desert light glaring off the gray tiles. Carefully smiling, I lifted my head. But only suspicious female faces regarded me from behind the pillars. As long as I had been with Keith, I realized, I was cloaked in Western privilege, but as I walked toward the women's section, looking for Mehmet's wife, I felt this privilege shearing off, bit by bit. With Keith I was a tourist, an object of curiosity. But alone, with neither a husband nor a child to validate me, I became an unknown woman, possibly a prostitute, an unclean object, profane.

I saw Mehmet's wife hurrying toward me; she took me by the hand and led me to a colonnade at the rear of the courtyard, in the shade. She bustled me to her mat, amid hundreds of mats laid out side by side in a patchwork down the platform. The women sat cross-legged on the ground, leaning toward each other and talking, their white, green, or black scarves knotted tightly across their throats. When I sat with them, one of the women scooted away, mumbling "*Haram!*"

I would hear this word over and over in the next hour: *Haram*, with an admonitory weight on the second syllable. I later learned this word means "forbidden," but at the time I knew only that the women began to cluster around me, tugging the elbow-length sleeves of the cloak down to cover my wrists, pushing at stray hairs that wisped from my scarf, pulling the flap of the robe over my bare ankle. I came to understand: *I am forbidden*. Their hands touched me all over, patting me into place; under these hands I felt like a very small child, or a doll made of damp, still pliant, clay.

Even in my discomfort, I knew I felt only a bit of what these women endured all their lives: numerous hands pressing them into a posture of shame, submission, invisibility. If my family had been orthodox Jews, I would have been molded the same way, shunted away from the men, bundled into a scarf, taught to keep my gaze fixed on the ground. The shame of being a woman, the dangerous sorcery of the body concealed: I would have learned these things had I been a devout follower of my own religion.

Finally the prayers began and the women turned their attention to the muezzin. At varying intervals they stood to pray, bowing from the waist, hands on knees, then kneeling on the mat, head to the ground, arms outstretched, then up again, over and over. I looked down the row and saw hundreds of women praying, their robes layered at the hips, wafting a vague a scent of olive soap and laundered cotton. Mehmet's wife, with a wave of her hand and a lift of her eyebrows, asked me to pray with her. But I shrugged and shook my head. Would it be more sacrilegious to mimic the movements of prayer, or to sit in a posture of respectful silence? "I don't know how to pray," I said in English, surprised to hear a catch in my voice. *Afwan*, I said. *Excuse me.* Sweat ran down my neck, across my abdomen. Some of the women finished early, rushing through the movements, and again they inched closer, touching me, pushing my hair back under the hood. *Haram*, they muttered, *Haram*.

On another cue, unheard, the women stood again. I saw men wandering in and out of the courtyard, some fanning themselves as they reclined near the door of the shrine. I stood up and saw, far across the courtyard, Keith laughing with Mehmet. What could they be discussing? Politics? Family? Food? I yearned to be with them, to be exempt from the rules of women, away from these women's hands. But Mehmet's wife pulled me back from the ledge. She again motioned, this time a little more forcefully, for me to pray.

So I did. I bent, placed my hands on my knees, and tried to feel something, anything resembling a prayer. I followed Mehmet's wife, moving my hands, my head, my lips. I hardly remembered praying in my own synagogue, mumbling along beside my mother and father, tired and hot and hungry, smelling the stale odors of mothballs and Emeraude, prune Danish and Folgers coffee. I remembered sitting at my Hebrew school desk while the teacher called the roll, and my own name—*Basha Leah*—ringing in my ears. I liked Basha Leah. I created a persona for her, an amalgam of Bible stories from Miriam to

Ruth. *Basha Leah* drank from a sacred well. *Basha Leah* danced for the children. *Basha Leah* was cool and elegant, with wise eyes and a compassionate heart.

So, as *Basha Leah*, I prayed with Mehmet's wife—I straightened up, rocked a little on my heels, then sank to my knees and pressed my forehead to the ground. Here I could see nothing; the hood of my cloak shrouded me, blotted out the light. I faced Mecca, my arms outstretched, my head bowed in an attitude of respect and devotion. Millions of Muslims faced Mecca that same moment, sending the force of their worship in this direction, their prayers rolling over the slope of my Jewish back.

I don't know how long I stayed like this—face down, my back a shell, my eyes shut tight. But soon I heard the rustle and swish of robes, children querying their mothers for food. I sat up, my face flushed with heat. The women seemed to have forgotten me as they gathered up their mats and yelled for the children who chased each other among the pillars. A young man circulated through the women's section, selling sesame-studded bread from a stick. Mehmet's wife sat placidly next to me, her hands intertwined in her lap.

I wanted to tell Mehmet's wife I was Jewish. I also wanted to explain that I'd never been bat-mitzvahed; I was a Jewish girl, I would say, but I didn't feel like a Jewish woman. I wanted to tell her I could not bear children of my own, and so my future as a woman remained uncertain: how would I fit myself into a family history, into the traditions of my own religion? I thought she might raise her eyebrows, but she wouldn't grow angry; I thought she might smile and say something kind to me in a language we could both understand.

But I remained silent, and in silence we waited until Mehmet came to fetch us away.

Next year in Jerusalem!

Keith and I pass through the gate into the old city of Jerusalem, inching our way through the crowded bazaar. There are dried apricots and peaches, huge bins of garbanzo beans, stacks of green soap, chunks of lamb smoking on spits. Boys careen down the steep alleyways with laden carts, braking by crushing their heels against a dangling rubber tire. We step over a threshold to the Jewish quarter.

The air clears; the crowd thins; spotless windows frame gold-chunk bracelets, silver amulets, hand-painted silk. The walls are a golden-hued sandstone; tract lighting glows from the ceiling. A gaggle of teen-aged girls swarms by us, followed by an escort, a man with a revolver bulging in his pocket. I see a woman browsing in a jewelry store; she's wearing a flowered-print dress, sandals, and an automatic rifle casually slung over her shoulder. A cluster of machine guns leans against a shop window; a tourist poses with an M-16 in front of a synagogue.

As if following a trail by memory, or instinct, we're drawn to a terrace overlooking the Wailing Wall. When I was a child in Hebrew school, they showed us black-and-white newspaper photos of Hasidic men *davening* against this wall, women crying, bar-mitzvah boys hugging the Torah. My teachers spoke of the worshippers leaning so close to the stone they kissed it. The photos must have been snapped from exactly this angle: the Dome of the Rock rising in the background, and in the foreground the ruined gray wall, with its rough-cut stones and moss growing from between the cracks. And, flush to the wall, the swaying line of worshippers. As a child I thought this was the place a Jew came when he was sad and needed to cry.

When my family held their wine glasses aloft and pledged, *Next year in Jerusalem!*, they had exactly this place in mind. The men saw themselves in tallis and yarmulkes, joining Jews from around the world in a steady chant. The women imagined rejoining their mothers and grandmothers in song. Jerusalem and the Wailing Wall were identical.

Keith and I pass through a police checkpoint and hurry down the steps into the courtyard. As if by instinct, I glance up at the rim of the wall for snipers. Two police vans glide into the enclosure; a cadre of soldiers clatters down the steps, and we blend into the crowd of tourists swarming toward the wall. On one side are the men, the dark mass of Hasidic Jews on the far left, rocking rhythmically; on the other side the women mill in muted dresses and scarves. A few people sit away from the wall in dull gray folding chairs, but most are packed shoulder to shoulder along the stones.

What am I to do, now that I'm here in the land of my grandfather's imagination? Keith leans down and whispers in my ear. "We'll meet up in a bit." He wanders to the men's side, and I see a gatekeeper drop a cardboard yarmulke onto his head.

A woman approaches me as I enter the women's section. "Are you Jewish?" she says. Her face is neutral, composed. "Yes," I say, "I'm Jewish." But the woman squints at me and continues her interrogation, unconvinced. "Is your mother Jewish?" she asks, her gaze roaming across my forehead, my nose, my mouth. "Yes, my mother is Jewish," I meekly reply. She smiles approvingly and hands me a blank slip of paper.

Then I see them—the prayers rolled up and stuck into cracks, falling in drifts at the foot of the wall. To my left, I hear the sing-song voices of the men, murmuring, and above that the occasional throaty calls of the black-hatted Hasids bowing back and forth, their foreheads tapping the wall. The Hebrew sounds familiar as English, though I have no idea what it means. I watch the women on my side:

their palms flat on the wall, their heads bent, their lips moving in mumbled devotion.

I've read the Wailing Wall is an ear to God, and that's why so many come to touch it, to press their lips against the mossy rocks. I watch the women reading *sotto voce* from their prayer books, or sometimes with no voice at all, just moving their lips and rocking back and forth on their heels. Eventually I get close enough to touch a tentative finger to the stone. This one brick is wider than my arms spread side-to-side; the surface buckles and curves. This was a stone laid down by King Herod's men, before the birth of Christ. It feels cool and comforting, and I would keep my hand there longer, but I back off quickly to allow a small woman in a gray scarf to take her desperate place at the wall.

From the men's section I hear one of the Hasids, his prayer warbling high above the muted voices, and one of the women next to me, her hands covering her eyes, cries out in response. I back away, as I see the other women have done, keeping the wall in sight. I've said no prayer, not even to myself; I've written no plea to the *shekinah* who resides within the stones.

But even as I shuffle in humiliation away from the wall, I know on my last day in Jerusalem I'll feel compelled to revisit the courtyard alone. I'll take my place, leaning forward to touch my forehead against the wall. I might hold both palms flat against the rock. I'll smell moss and dust and the stone that still molders beneath the earth. I'll smell the breath of millions of women before me, and I'll smell the skin of the woman next to me, her lips moving, her eyes tightly closed. Prayer has an odor of devotion and righteousness, but here it's also the smell of milk and mothballs, scarves folded in a drawer, and seltzer for the grandchildren in big glass bottles next to the fridge. It's the sound of children fidgeting at the table as they listen to the stories over and over, chewing on matzoh and *haroses*. It's the sound of my mother dishing up the brisket, the roast chicken. I'll smell my grandmother, the powder behind her ears, and I'll hear my grandfather mumbling his prayer on the other side, a voice perilously close to song.

I don't know if I'll write anything down, commit my voice to a parchment scroll and leave it forever in one of the empty cracks. But I'll know how to pray. I'll turn my head slightly and press my ear to listen against the stone.

A Different Person

The Bridge

In Amman, giant Pepsi cans rotate on the roofs of bus stations, Kellogg's corn flakes line the market shelves, and I can buy Neutrogena soap in a mall. I can taste homemade ice cream in a hundred different flavors—mango, chocolate, lemon, strawberry, coconut. After traveling for several weeks in the eastern stretches of Turkey and then down through Syria, I find such things decadent, almost hallucinatory. My boyfriend, Keith, and I have a room on the roof of Hotel Bader, where duct tape crisscrosses the windows. The city— enormous, chaotic—hums outside our door. From its highest building, they say, you can see the lights of Jerusalem.

It's July 1994, and the Gaza Strip and Jericho have just been given Palestinian self-rule. Yasir Arafat's trip to Jericho has been postponed, rescheduled several times. The *Jordan Times* reports shootings in the old city of Jerusalem, a buildup of hostility in Jericho. Tanks rumble in the streets, and the border between Jordan and the West bank has been closed several times.

Before we had entered Syria, Keith bought me a brass wedding ring, a prop. He bargained the woman down to 30 cents, then he slipped the ring on my grimy finger. All through the journey, I've been polishing the ring with my thumb to give it the aspect of gold. We both know that this trip will be the last one we'll take together; at the end of it we'll separate for the final time. He'll return to Turkey, where he teaches English; I'll return to Seattle alone.

My wedding ring is not the only fabrication: On the visa form I identified myself as a married, Christian teacher, traveling only for the purposes of tourism. Only later did I fully comprehend that to put down "Jewish" might have barred us from the country; only later did I know that a Jewish woman who finds her way to Israel via Arab lands will be an ambivalent tourist, indeed. At the time, I acted only from the instinct that told me I could no longer travel as myself.

Now that we're in Jordan, only a few miles from the border, my desire to see Jerusalem has become irrational, one that feels like hunger. I feel the tug on my chest; I know I'll never be this close again. But I'm not really an adventurous traveler. And the news reports make me nervous. Keith is the adventurous one; he'll go anywhere with good cheer. He picks up languages easily and chats with whoever sits beside him. People give him gifts without provocation. Me, I tend to remain silent, wary, turning my face away when a stranger approaches.

To get more information about the situation in Israel, we visit the American Embassy, a sprawling complex on the outskirts of Amman. It looks like a Marriott hotel, with ochre tiles in the courtyard, picture windows, an art gallery, air-conditioning. A jeep with a revolving machine gun patrols outside the fence. Inside, we sit in the waiting room with an expatriate who claims to be an advisor to the royal family in Saudi Arabia. He peers at us through thick, grease-coated glasses, clutching a well-worn file in his hands.

Bulletins dated a week earlier urge travelers to use extreme caution and to cross the border only if necessary. "So does that mean we shouldn't go now?" Keith asks the woman behind the glass.

She shrugs. It's up to us, she says. The situation is always changing.

We linger a while in the air-conditioning, undecided, studying the black-and-white photographs of ancient Arab women, Bedouins riding camels, wide-eyed Jordanian children.

"You're safe with me," Keith says.

"I know. But what if you get sick? What if you get hit by a car?"

He picks up my hand. On this hand I'm wearing the wedding ring, and he twists it around my finger.

"If I get hit by a car," Keith says, "you would become a different person."

I know what he means. He means that we make choices—in travel, in relationships. The way we stand in proximity to the world is not static but governed by decisions we make moment to moment. I've chosen to be afraid, because I know Keith will act unafraid and strong. I've allowed myself to be shy, because I know Keith will make friends for us. I have chosen to be silent, because I know Keith will collect the words we need to know.

"I promise," he says, "not to get us into anything dangerous. First sign of trouble and we're out of there."

The King Hussein Bridge out of Jordan to the West Bank was closed yesterday, but today, the taxi driver tells us, it's bound to be open. Arafat has passed through Gaza; in response, a riot erupted at Damascus Gate in Jerusalem—a mob of right-wing Jews threw stones, breaking most of the shop windows in the Arab-owned shops lining Nablus Road. Curfews have been imposed. I pack our crossing permit in my money belt—a piece of paper with seventeen names typed on it in English and Arabic, along with a few official purple stamps. According to the Jordanians, we are still in Jordan when we cross to the West Bank. According to the Israelis we are in Israel, and they will stamp us in. Officially, we'll be in two countries at once.

Miracles

Our first night in Jerusalem, and we're staying inside the walls of the old city, in a hostel up from the Arab Bazaar. Keith has a craving for beer. It's dark out, but not too late, about 8:00. We go down the steps and out into the night.

The bazaar is empty and dark, all the stalls shut behind steel doors. No lights. Not a sound. The shadowy alley stretches out for a hundred yards before us, then abruptly turns a corner. It's as if the bazaar never existed; not even a smell of falafel remains. The Arabs have vanished as if vaporized. The damp street smells faintly of wet clay.

We start walking in the direction of Damascus Gate. Last night, we heard, there was a riot in the courtyard. Some people told us they watched it from the balcony of their hostel: crowds of Israelis throwing stones and shattering shop windows, the Palestinians held at bay by the guns of the Israeli soldiers. Shots were fired, but no one was hit.

A group of Palestinian boys appears around the bend, herded by six Israeli soldiers. We flatten ourselves against a wall, and the group jostles past us, the boys sticking their chests out, strutting, and the soldiers trotting after them, silent, their guns held in the position of fire. As they pass us, one of the soldiers does a quick turn on his heel, sweeping the nose of his rifle in an arc across the alleyway.

Soldiers are everywhere, but an Arab man walks calmly, holding an infant in his arms. The steps up to the gate are lit slightly by the moon, but we must turn a corner before heading outside the wall, a corner dark even during the day, now pitch black. Two soldiers peer down from the wall into the courtyard, their guns at the ready under their arms.

I want to be a different person. But I am a Jewish girl who grew up in the comfortable suburbs of Los Angeles. I have never heard a mortar round, a bomb, or a gunshot. So I talk Keith into returning to our hostel, where we go up on the roof to see Jerusalem spread out beneath us: the Dome of the Rock drawing the eye, where Mohammed is said to have placed his last step before ascending to Heaven; and below that the Western Wall, site of the Jewish Temple built by Solomon and destroyed by the Romans; and beyond that the garden of Gethsemane, with the Russian Orthodox Church domes rising from the olive trees, where Jesus is said to have preached love to his disciples. To the south we see Mount Zion, where Mary left the earth, and where King David may have been buried. And behind us: the spires rise from the Church of the Holy Sepulcher, one of the sites of Jesus's tomb.

Strands of electric wires and telephone lines weave a net across the roofs of the old city. In the alley below us we hear a shot, or maybe it was a backfire?, and then another. A couple of shouts, then nothing. From this distance the city is beautiful, the way a memory is beautiful, stripped of the mundane details of survival. From here, I can see how the Western Wall is common with the Temple Mount; on one side, the Jews whisper to God and mourn their history; on the other side, Muslim women and children sit gazing in to a peaceful garden.

Earlier in the day, at the citadel of David, with the blue-and-white Israeli flags flapping in the wind, I saw a dove, then two and three. They flew from the walls and nestled into the dense branches of the olive trees and the date palms, their backs a phosphorescent blue. With wings outspread and tails fanned, they look exactly like the dove of peace adorning the official map of Israel, the olive branch dangling from her beak.

Or maybe they weren't doves at all but common pigeons. I remember the pet pigeons on the neighboring roof outside our window at the Hotel Cairo in Syria. We watched a man wave a stick, on which he had tied a white flag; he waved it around and around above his head to keep the birds flying in formation. Then he lowered the wand and allowed the birds to flutter down and feed from his hand. He glanced up and saw us watching; he waved and shouted *Merhaba! Welcome! Hello!*

The Language

Keith and I have moved to Cairo Hostel, in the Arab section just outside Damascus Gate. Most of the clientele are young British travelers on their way to or from Egypt, strands of hair wrapped in blue and yellow yarn.

We have a room and a balcony to ourselves, and we sit there in the mornings, eating yogurt and corn flakes bought from the grocer next door. I bring home Jewish pastries from the market, layered crescents of butter and chocolate and cinnamon. We eat pickled herring and cream cheese on chewy flat bread and scoop out chunks of smoked salmon from plastic take-out containers. We eat latkes stuffed in a pita with French fries, and falafel with minted yogurt. We eat Arabic pizza with egg and tomato on top.

On Friday, Keith and I shower, put on the best clothes we can muster from our backpacks, and head toward the Wailing Wall. Giddiness fills the air like a party. A group of men dances backward, singing, their arms looped together. Our escort to Shabbat dinner is supposed to be a short man in saddle shoes. I finally spy the shoes, glaring white in the mass of black wingtips and sneakers. It takes nearly an hour to sort out the groups, who's going where. "Are you with the Goldblums?" "No, I'm with Katz."

We get to the Rabbi's house, a small apartment in a well-groomed complex. The small room is already packed with people, and as we enter the Rabbi calls for his wife to "bring more chairs! Where are the chairs?" He looks like the rabbi at my childhood temple, a large man with an archaic smile on his lips, a beard, big meaty hands. He enlists several men to carry a sofa outside to make room for more tables, more chairs. There must be close to sixty people sitting shoulder to shoulder in the room. Beyond their heads I can see the wall-length shelves of books, and a phalanx of flickering candles, and silk wall hangings reading "Shalom." I could be in my cousin Murray's house in Van Nuys, the family assembling for Passover. Somehow we find places to sit at a table, and someone offers Keith a yarmulke and a bobby pin.

The rabbi's wife is a small woman, with glowing cheeks, carrying a baby at her hip. She pushes a bulky white scarf around on her head as she bustles between kitchen and dining room. I find out later that she is my age, thirty-five, and she has ten children, and every Shabbat they host a dinner like this, never knowing how many people will show up. "It's what I do," she says, smiling. "It's my way of giving back a little." She and her husband are from Brooklyn, near where my mother grew up.

Finally we are ready to begin. Then a few more diners bustle through the door, settlers from Gaza; they carry automatic rifles and rounds of extra ammunition. Chairs are found for them; the guns are passed from hand to hand over the table to rest against the wall.

"I'm sorry," the rabbi begins. "I apologize for the crowded conditions here. One of you has already left because he did not feel comfortable in my house. I may never see this person again, I wish him well, I feel terrible and I apologize for any discomfort."

We begin a collective murmur of protest, but he silences us with his hand, and begins the prayer over the bread. Three enormous *challas* sit under embroidered white cloths at the center of the table. He cuts them with swift expertise, sawing first in half crosswise, then cutting through the whole length, then chopping up into chunks. We're starving. We wait patiently for the bread as it's passed around the table. We ladle gefilte fish onto our plates, and carrots and roast chicken. The platters keep appearing, and bottles of soda water and grape juice. This is the food of my childhood, dinners eaten for hours while the cousins shouted each other down and told jokes and cackled with laughter.

As the food circles the tables, Rabbi Goldblum sits back in his chair, a child on either side, a child in his lap, and begins to tell us a story. "This is the beginning of the month of Av," he says. "A dark month for the Jewish people. A month of mourning. It was in the month of Av that the temple was destroyed. It was also in this month that Aaron died. And who was Aaron? Aaron was the older brother of Moses."

I remember the tomb of Aaron beckoning from the mountain in Jordan, the tiny flash of white adobe in the sun. "We don't hear about Aaron so much," the Rabbi continues, "because Moses was such a big shot. But was Aaron jealous of his brother's success? No, he was not a jealous man. Aaron was a peacemaker. He would go to both parties in a disagreement; he would tell a little white lie to each one; and everyone would be satisfied. His death signaled an end to the harmony among the different peoples of the world."

The rabbi tells us the custom in his household at Shabbat is for everyone to tell something about themselves, to offer a little bit of wisdom. "I may never see you again," he says, spreading his arms wide, "and I want to connect the faces and the names. I want to remember you. But one thing I ask—please, no politics. If politics is the most important knowledge you have to offer, please, tonight, give us the second most important knowledge you have."

So we began to eat, and the voices emerge from around the room, some telling complex Talmudic stories, some offering just a fragment of their personal history. One young man tells us the story of his sister, who has just begun treatments for skin cancer. His moral: "Stay out of the sun." The rabbi—who remains in constant motion throughout the meal, dishing out food for his children, comforting the child in his lap, filling glasses—he listens carefully to everyone and says thank you before moving on.

After about forty-five minutes, it's Keith's turn. He sits forward in his chair. "I want to say that where we have traveled in Syria and Jordan," I feel a prickle of suspicion rise in the room, "we encountered wonderful acts of generosity and a true desire for peace. And the hospitality offered to us here tonight makes me think that peace may truly be possible." The rabbi thanks him quickly and turns to me.

I've been practicing a speech, but now all language evaporates. "I am the first person in my family to make it to Jerusalem," I stutter. "And I didn't plan to come here at all." The room is silent; my heart pounds in my ears. I can think of nothing else to offer, nothing but the fact of my pilgrimage here through the Arab countries, nothing but a faint testimony to the kindness of the Syrians. But I remain silent, so the rabbi thanks me and goes on to the person on my right, a woman who is divorcing her husband in order to make her home in Israel.

By the time we finish dinner, it's after midnight. "Where are you staying?" someone asks.

"At Cairo Hostel."

"Where?"

"Near Damascus Gate."

He gestures toward the settlers from Gaza, who are clipping on their ammunition. These men speak to no one; they are pale and gaunt, their movements quick. "You better go back with these guys," he says. "They're loaded."

I know the Jews who live in Jerusalem have reason to be afraid. I know I would not walk through the Arab sections, alone, with a yarmulke on my head, in the dark. But I want to tell this man about the five-course meals I shared in the houses of friendly Syrians, about visiting mosques and praying along with the Muslim worshippers, about eating *schwarma* in the street bazaars and barely paying for a thing because the Syrians insisted on giving us everything for free. I want to tell him that I think I have come to know something essential about human nature, but in reality I know nothing. Still, this man facing me demands some kind of answer.

"I feel safer without the guns," I say.

"Oh, that's right. You guys have been to Syria. You know how to speak the language." And he turns his back to me before I can think of a reply.

Happiness

Jericho. We take a shared taxi through the desert, passing vast areas cordoned off by barbed wire which enclose shanties made of plywood, dirty canvas tents. "Refugee camps," one of the other passengers tells us, a Jordanian woman who works for the World Bank. She's on assignment to help work out the financial troubles of the fledgling Palestinian government.

"That must be difficult," Keith says, meaning it must be hard for a people who have long been without a government to suddenly find themselves in charge.

"Yes," she answers. "Appointments mean nothing to them. I can never find anyone in."

We take a winding road down into a river valley and arrive in the green oasis town, which displays vivid remnants of Arafat's visit. Sophisticated graffiti splashes across every wall: murals of Arafat bursting triumphantly through a barbed wire fence, holding the two ends in his fists; lurid portraits of Arafat in full military dress, laminated in glossy reds, yellows and khaki green. Hundreds of Palestinian flags flutter from wires strung across the main square.

Two Palestinian policemen, unarmed, stand nonchalantly on the corner, grinning. *Welcome*, they say. They shake Keith's hand.

"Are you happy?" we ask.

They laugh. "Yes, we are very happy," they say.

We wander through the town, and we sit and eat some ice cream in the shade. We take a snapshot of an immense flowering Judas tree, its red petals nearly obliterating the green leaves. Keith leans down and picks a bright sticker out of the gutter; it's the NBC peacock, fallen from the camera of a news teams following Arafat.

I thought Jericho would be tense with anticipated violence or the memory of violence just passed. But the only indication of such violence are some old photographs tacked up in a mercantile—black-and-white documentary shots of a riot, with Israeli tanks in the street, men running in all directions.

I feel oddly safe in Jericho. I don't want to go back to Jerusalem. I don't want to bear the responsibility, the history, or the sorrow that being a Jew in Jerusalem demands.

A Different Person

It's our last night together in Jerusalem. On the roof of the hostel, some kids play guitar while the lights of the city brighten. It's warm, the night air silky with Bible stories and miracles. Right across the street, they say, Jesus rose from the tomb. I have a picture of Keith emerging from the cave, waving among the onlookers.

The kids are playing "Guinevere" and I want to dance. For a moment Keith and I waltz awkwardly in place, then sway for a few moments, looking at the view. "Guinevere had green eyes," a young man croons off-key, "like you, baby, like you." I think of being alone here for a day and automatically start to plan all my movements— through the Arab quarter, where I'll try to bargain for souvenirs, to the Western Wall, where I will bow my head against the stone and pray. I won't be too frightened because I'll know my way around. I'll know where I can go and where I cannot.

Keith and I go downstairs to our room with the arched windows, the palms outside rustling in the wind. I take off the fake wedding ring and stand a moment at the window. The ring has left a faint discoloration on my finger, and I feel light without it, light in a way that could signal either liberation or terror. Already I'm drawn into the flow of departure: the bus starting up, the twisted lanes of passport control, the last glimpse of a head as it turns away. Already I feel like a different person, but what exactly has changed, I could never tell you for sure.

I Need a Miracle

I'm twenty years old, sitting in my parents' living room in the San Fernando Valley, trying to translate my favorite eight-track tapes to cassette for my drive up north. I'm starting over, going to college in Arcata after a few detours that left me stranded back home, a daughter again, under my parents' roof. Playing Grateful Dead, Neil Young, Heart—all those anthems I listen to in the privacy of my bedroom, my car, the songs cranking me open, and now here I am, with my father, exposed. Bob Weir's belting out the Dead's "I Need a Miracle," and the lyrics make me blush: "*I need a woman 'bout twice my height / Statuesque, raven-dressed, a goddess of the night. . . .*"

My father doesn't seem to notice: he kneels on the shag carpet, focused intently on how the music might get transferred from one kind of tape to another without too much distortion. For him, it's a technical problem, not an emotional one. My father's an engineer, and he has figured out some system to do this—perhaps we've angled the machines toward one another, at just the right distance, so the music will fly through the space between and be captured without interference. Or maybe he's hooked up some cables, has it all figured out. In any case, I remember having to be very quiet, to make sure none of the sounds of everyday life—my mother washing dishes in the next room, the scuffle of our knees on the carpet—slip accidentally into the mix.

I know I'm already scripting that drive up north, the way the Dead will accompany me as a soundtrack, making it all feel like a quest rather than the halting and bumbling transition it is. I think of my father kneeling with me, and all around us the music to which I had danced high on acid, music to which I'd made love in the rain, music that had shimmied in my blood like narcotics . . . and here is my dad fiddling with the machines, not saying a word, but just trying to help his daughter find the armor that might protect her as she ventures out again into the world.

Something goes wrong, I don't know what, and I blurt out *shit!* He looks up, so startled and hurt. I say *sorry, but this is* important *to me*, in that way I had back then, so absorbed in the trappings of my own life I had little regard for others. He says, *I know, I know, be patient, we'll get it right.* And he keeps at it, slips the thick black box of the eight-track into its player, synchronizes it with the slim cassette player, each of us quiet, quiet, looking into each other's eyes, his finger on *record*, my finger poised on *play*.

"A Touch of Grey," "Althea," "Uncle John's Band": all my favorite songs built to a moment when the music itself disappeared and we floated on a raft the music left behind. . . . *And it's real and it won't go away, oh no / I can't get around and I can't run away.* . . . we felt the Dead playing us, teasing us into a realm where the dead and the living co-abide, a world where no judgment exists, no striving, no pain, only your pure self stripped bare. . . . *Too much of everything is just enough / One more thing I just got to say / I need a miracle every day!* The

Dead knew how to create chaos and then a clear path out of that chaos; they knew how to break you and put you back together again.

But how could I explain any of this to my father, as he knelt beside me on the carpet, in a home filled with carefully manicured plants, the smell of roast chicken from the night before, the ceramic *Shalom* hanging cheerfully on the wall in the entry? This man whose inner self I had never glimpsed, or bothered to glimpse, only looked at him sideways as I slid out the door. I got a fleeting glance of him in his recliner, the big ashtray beside him on the oak end table while the Lakers flickered on the television. I thought I had nothing in common with him, that he would never understand me, that I was superior to him because I had found *this* music, because music had redeemed me.

But now, over thirty years later, I see a father reaching out to his daughter in the way he knows best: through fiddling with a technology that has outlived its novelty, the eight-tracks already clumsy in comparison to the sleek and light cassettes that have replaced them. He is helping his daughter transcribe the music she loves from one medium to another, both of these recordings dependent on magnetism to catch and inscribe sound forever. My dad and I knelt for hours on the carpet, and we watched the music unfurl from one to the other, and the Dead sang it again and again: "*I need a miracle, I need a miracle, I need a miracle every day.*"

That's how I felt when I was eighteen, and nineteen, and twenty: that the world needed to offer miracles to me continuously, that I deserved them, and they could never be forthcoming in this living room, with this father, and with this mother making lunch out of sight, with these brothers who seemed to hate me, with this neighborhood and its studious conformity—each tract home gazing blandly at its neighbor, the children circling the block, the sedans driving the speed limit up the cul-de-sacs, these dead-end streets. No, I thought miracles could only be found on the open road, music blaring out the windows, the many tracks of my life converging in a flash of harmony.

But now I see it, the miracle that had been there all along: my father kneeling with me, that house holding me safe until I decided not to be safe anymore. I didn't yet know that I'd leave that house and stumble into an affair with an alcoholic, that I'd waste the rest of my college years trying to console a man who would not be consoled. That I'd listen to the Grateful Dead for hours on those cassettes in a dark room by myself, the music steadily losing its power to redeem. I'd get pregnant, have a miscarriage, and I'd keep listening, wishing I could hear a trace of my father or my mother in the background, a stray memory of home.

But for now, I just want the music to transfer cleanly, purely, and I'm kneeling with my father, fiddling with the controls. Behind us sits my parents' heavy console with its turntable hidden beneath a little door, and all the records my parents love lined up in their sleeves: the soundtrack to *West Side Story*, or Herb Alpert and the Tijuana Brass, with its cover of a woman swathed in a wedding dress made only of whipped cream. As a child I used to stare at that cover for hours, wondered how it felt to wear something so cool and sweet, a dress that could dissolve in an instant. I wondered how she looked so pure and yet so naughty in her shroud of evaporating white.

I wish I could hear it again, all of it: Herb Alpert on the turntable, the brass instruments warbling their pleasure, while my parents sit in their matching recliners, smiling uncertainly at me as I slip out the door. Jerry Garcia crooning from the stage—*I told Althea I was feeling lost / Lacking in some direction* . . . his lips kissing the microphone—or Bob Weir belting out, *I need a miracle every day!* And I want to hear it with the ears of someone who is twenty years old and just learning to pray, someone who believes in transcendence, a girl who knows that all worship rises first in the body, peeling away all obstacles until the world becomes clear and still. But such a thing, I know, is impossible, because that girl no longer exists, and Jerry Garcia died of a heart attack, and the Dead are gone, dispersed. Herb Alpert is gone and so are the eight-track tapes, and even the cassettes that always ended up catching and pulling out in a mess of long black ribbons that could no longer sing. The music I listen to now arrives out of nowhere, ephemeral, and there's no way my dad could catch it for me, there's no way he can bend on his now-replaced knees and say, *Don't worry sweetheart, we'll figure it out, we'll be sure to get it right.*

Blessing of the Animals

*You touch
the right one and a whole half of the universe
wakes up, a new half.*

—WILLIAM STAFFORD

Here's the first thing you should know:

When I sit next to my dog Abbe just before she falls asleep, and I stroke her fine-boned head, she turns just enough so that her nose somehow nuzzles between my wrist and my sleeve. She breathes in some scent she's found there—perhaps the smell of my pulse. I keep my hand very still then, her nose glued to my wrist as she snuffles and sighs. The whole house goes quiet, all of us just breathing: the couch and the cat, the vase and the tulips, the mirror and the broom. All of us just here, just now, in the trance of a dog who knows nothing, yet, but grace.

That's the first thing you should know.

But let's start in church, a Unitarian church a mile from my house— white siding and the requisite signboard out front posted with fine, literary sayings printed on massive sheets of paper. I have a postcard of one of those signs I've kept for years pinned to my bulletin board: "You are constantly invited to be what you are"—Emerson. For some reason, it's just the message I need more times than most, this permission to be myself. I've passed by the Bellingham church many times and attended a few secular events there, though I've never gone to a service. But I like the Unitarians, with their cheerful sense of justice, and I even considered myself a pseudo-Unitarian/Jew/Buddhist when I lived for a time in Salt Lake City.

Now, many years later in Bellingham, I've read a notice in the paper about the annual "Blessing of the Animals" ceremony this Sunday. And because Abbe is six months old, and because she is full of vast enthusiasm for any enterprise that involves new people and dogs, and because I'm still in that eager New Dog Owner phase where I'm delighted for any opportunity to show off my puppy, I gather her collar and her leash, her treats and poop bags, her water bottle and bowl; I give her a quick brush down as she turns herself in tight circles, trying to grab the brush's handle in her mouth. "We have to look nice for church," I say, in that mothering tone I've taken to so easily, too easily, my voice a little hoarse from constantly being elevated to such a high, unfamiliar pitch.

At the last minute I remember my cat, Madrona, and since it would not be a blessing to cart her to church, I quickly print off my favorite picture of her: she kneels on my improvised altar, paws tucked beneath her chest, a tiny brass Buddha in the foreground— just being her prickly, bodhisattva self. She often paces into that room when I'm sitting, brushes the full side of her body against the curve of my crossed legs until I pet her once or twice, then she settles down on the altar, assuming her place as a deity to be worshipped.

No one has to invite her to be what she is. My cat knows she's bigger than the Buddha, that she could kick Buddha's ass if it came down to it, and I've often entered this room to find that serene little figure knocked on its side, his tiny hands still formed in a perfect mudra of peace.

Here's the second thing you should know:

I've had only one other dog in my life, a Great Dane named Sheba. Tall, of course, with a smooth brindled coat, but I couldn't truthfully tell you her color, because I remember this dog only in black and white. All the photos, gray-scale: Sheba, a puppy still, a silhouette in the barren backyard of my parents' new home, circa 1960, in the nascent suburbs of the San Fernando Valley. Soon there will be tall eucalyptus trees, a Doughboy swimming pool, a jungle gym that starts to rust the moment it's assembled, but for now there's just this skinny big dog, a newly planted lawn, some saplings lined up by the fence.

I can't yet talk, can't yet walk; in the photos I'm just a blob of a being with big eyes and a spit curl quivering on the top of my bulbous head. After my father drinks his Ovaltine and his Tang and goes to work, it's just me and my mother and my 3-year-old brother and this big lanky dog—a pack of four in the clean new house, wondering what to do with ourselves.

The dog doesn't wonder too hard. She knows her job: to protect us all from whatever dangers present themselves. She follows my mother everywhere—from kitchen to bathroom to bedroom to yard. She barks at the sedans cruising up our cul-de-sac, cocks her head with suspicion when the phone rings. She nudges the little baby in my mother's arms when she cries.

That baby eventually begins to grow, to leave her mother's arms and get down on the floor to crawl, to walk, to run. This puts her at eye level with the dog more times than not, and Sheba herds her around the green shag carpet, places her body between the baby and the screen door to the patio. The dog is just the right height for a toddler to pat with her fist, to pull herself up, to walk under the arch-way of those enormous knees. Eventually this girl will haul herself onto Sheba's back, squeal *giddyup!*, and the dog will comply, moving slowly, swaying like a camel. When the girl is ill, she'll recline into Sheba's belly, both of them licking salt off their upper lips. Both of them will feel relieved when the fever has passed.

When I'm eight years old, my family (which by now includes a baby brother) will go on vacation somewhere, a long car trip to a place like Carlsbad Caverns or Sea World or Sequoia National Park. Sheba is too big to go, so we leave her at a boarding kennel, and I remember watching for too long the closed gray doors of that kennel from the way back of the station wagon as we pulled away.

For some reason, I remember that Sheba dies while we're gone. I remember driving up to the kennel; I remember the heat waves rippling up from the black asphalt, waiting in the car as our father strides through those gray doors, then is gone longer than seems nec-essary. We roll down the windows, whine for ice cream; my mother fans herself with a map. My father finally appears, *sans* dog, his face white, his mouth set in a grim line of displeasure. He walks slowly, too slowly, back to the now silent car.

But now I know this whole scene is inaccurate, a figment of mem-ory. My mother tells me it all happened at home: alone in the house with Sheba, who is vomiting bile, everyone else at school or at work, my mother wrestles the 130 lb. dog into the car by herself, sobbing and cajoling, telling her it will be all right. She takes the dog to the vet, who calls later in the day to tell her Sheba has died, a twisted stomach, something that happens often to the big breeds. I must have come home from school—a school, where I'd recently been admonished *not* to sing the Star-Spangled Banner with my classmates because my voice was too off key; a school, where even the game of four-square had become dangerous, the heavy rubber ball bouncing with more force than necessary into my box; a school where my only solace was reading time, when I cocooned myself with words not my own. I must have come home, expecting to bend my whole body over Sheba's back and lie there, a rag doll, allowing school to subside, and instead saw my mother's distorted face, her eyes rimmed with smudged mascara. She must have told me, in whatever way you tell a child such things, that Sheba had been put to sleep.

Put to sleep. It's such a kind phrase, a gentle nudge. After all, I was put to sleep every night of my childhood, with kisses and hugs and promises of a good day tomorrow. And every morning, Sheba lifted her ponderous head, turned her caramel gaze on me as I woke. For those few moments—before the world rushed in to let me know its demands, to let me know I might not be up to snuff—I existed as nothing more than an object of adoration, a body to be loved.

That's the second thing you should know.

Let's return to church, or not even the church yet, but the parking lot, where already there's a certain giddiness in the air—*dogs in church!* Even for the short car ride, Abbe's curled herself onto the Navaho blanket and gone to sleep (she hates car rides and has learned quickly to simply pretend it's not happening, a skill I've come to wield in my own life as well), but as soon as the car stops she's up and wiggling in the back seat. Have I described her? She is a short-haired Havanese, a toy breed, with an apricot coat and a black-tipped, narrow snout. She looks, as most passersby comment, exactly like a miniature golden retriever, all fifteen pounds of her. My vet says it best: a golden retriever in a dachshund suit, with her short, slightly outturned legs, her triangular ears that flop over or stick straight up depending on her mood. Her eyes are dark and big and shaped like Spanish almonds.

As I clip on her leash and pull her from the car, I'm already watching out for other dogs—the border collies and huskies and goldens trotting up the sidewalk, pulling at their leashes. All the people smile, even those untethered. One woman comes up to me and says, "It's so nice to see who's coming to church today." I'm not sure if she means my dog or me, but it doesn't really matter—we're one unit, for now. Abbe, as she always does the minute she gets outside, has her nose to the ground, her legs pumping, sniffing away. She knows something's up, something that involves dogs and more dogs, and she couldn't really care less about me on the other end of this leash. When we get to the steps, I pick her up to take her inside.

Usually when I arrive at new places, I divert my gaze until I know what I'm supposed to do and when, who is safe to talk to and who is not. I'm always afraid of doing something wrong. But with Abbe in my arms I don't have to worry; most people look at her first anyway. She looks back and nudges them with her nose, sniffs deeply to find out who they are, finds everyone extremely worthy. In the vestibule, a mass of people with name tags turn our way, and exclaim over Abbe. They say how cute she is, what a good dog, and all I have to do is agree. Nothing else is required. Me, with all my complicated history, my jumbled disposition: I'm just an afterthought. It's as if I'm holding in my arms some small, furred portion of myself, a micro-me, who knows exactly who she is and where she belongs. This self radiates confidence, a word that means, in its purest form, simply to go with faith.

Here's another thing you should know:

For a long time, without quite knowing it, I blamed my parents. For years I kept that erroneous image of the boarding kennel in my head, and using kid logic, I suspected they had brought Sheba to the vet to die, that they had grown tired of her, that there had already been some kind of *arrangement* made, a notion I probably conceived from daytime television, hours of which I watched every day after school. It was not a suspicion I ever voiced, or even quite knew I carried, and my parents were gentle, loving people who would never do such a thing. But all I knew was: we never got another dog. Shortly after Sheba died, all three kids were trundled into the allergist's office and pricked with blunt square needles that reported our allergies to canines, cats, horses, ragweed, dust. We became a household without a dog, the backyard empty save for the Doughboy, the jungle gym, the now plush grass that rippled against the eucalyptus.

I still read books like a maniac. I read books while doing everything else, even walking down the street, even in the car, even though it made me sick. And I loved best dog stories, tales where the human and animal connection bordered on telepathy, where adventures escalated in thrall to those snouts sniffing the way ahead. I was dog-less, but dogs still accompanied me wherever I went.

Other animals appeared to fill the void. Most specifically, a family of gerbils, and one of them bit the palm of my hand so hard she hung there for several seconds while I screamed and whirled away. Another ate her babies right in front of me while I watched. There were turtles and hamsters and goldfish, none of which lasted long enough for me to form any attachment. There must have been other dogs on our street, but I have no memory of them; in my mind, our block becomes quiet and barren as a scene from the *Twilight Zone*. Sure, kids still roller-skated up and down the cul-de-sac. Sure, we still played hide-and-seek in the dusk. Sure, we still lived as a suburban family, and we crossed the empty field to the 7-11 for Slurpees, the sweet ice soothing our hot throats in the summertime. But something seemed missing, something had gone awry.

Then there was the duck. Why we had a white duck in our backyard is still a mystery, but there he is, swimming in the Doughboy pool, waddling beneath the walnut tree. Bright orange beak, marked with the hint of a smile, clacking open and closed. Webbed feet slapping the wet pavement. And quacking, quacking, quacking, as a duck is wont to do. I kind of loved him. We named him, not very imaginatively, "Daffy the Duck." His feathers were sleek and slightly oily, and he stretched out his neck and flapped his wings like an ungainly hummingbird when he saw you coming. I screeched open the back screen door first thing after coming home from school, and there he'd be, lifting himself out of a metal washbasin, waddling as fast as he could to greet me. While he was no Sheba, the quality and consistency of this greeting won me over, made the walk home from school more bearable.

But naturally the neighbors complained. All that honking! And at 5 A.M.! So one day we hoisted Daffy into the way back of the station wagon and brought him to the pond at Reseda Park. I'm sure I cried, because all the way there my father wove tales about how much *fun* the duck would have with his brethren, how he would make new friends *in no time at all*, how he would fly to *fabulous*, exotic places in the winter time. My mother nodded in agreement, but reached an arm over the front seat to pat me on the head, a gesture I took to be secret commiseration as much as consolation.

In the meantime, the duck fluttered and quacked and drew stares from the passing cars. He seemed quite happy, actually, to be on an outing, and kept poking his cool, heavy beak over the back seat to say hello. When we reached the park, we opened the tailgate, and he jumped out on his own, ruffled his feathers like an old lady straightening her bonnet, and immediately waddled toward the pond, where I could see dozens of non-descript ducks milling about the shore. We had brought a loaf of Wonder bread, and we wandered into the crowd like any other innocent park-goers, threw bits of bread to the assembled waterfowl. Our duck poked at the rim of the waterline, and we watched carefully to see when he would take off swimming.

Now! Once we thought Daffy happily occupied with his new home, we made our escape, strolling with exaggerated nonchalance to our car. *Don't look back*, my father said, that ancient edict, but of course I looked—I couldn't help myself. And there he was, *our* duck, waddling after us as fast as he could, head up high, wings splayed. He didn't look particularly distressed, no sense of *hey, where do you think you're going?* The beak still looked as though it were smiling, as if he were just heading back to the car with us on an unheard command.

He's following us! I yelled, and stopped in my tracks. *Just keep walking*, my father said, his face resolutely pointed forward. I know now he hated this, that we were probably doing something vaguely illegal, and that to leave an animal behind, no matter how misguided the impulse to keep him in the first place, would be anathema to him. But he was a father who needed to take care of something complicated in full view of his children. And he worked as an engineer, and like all good engineers he had come up with a plan, and we needed to work with it, to see it through.

I hesitated, stuck between an awkward love for this white, feathered creature and my love for my father, my fervent wish to ease his discomfort, to make everything *okay*. I was stuck between the imperative to keep walking, to move forward into the future where a duck in the backyard no longer existed, and my desire to stay a little bit longer in the past, where a duck feathered that yard and made me feel cherished. I knew I really had no choice; I was only a child, with a child's distorted sense of obligation. So I did both. I took a quick run back in the duck's direction, flapping my arms, shouting *shoo, shoo, shoo*, and he appeared truly startled—Daffy looked up at me with his beak open, wings frozen mid-flap, and I knew he understood that everything between us had changed. He backed down to the pond, his waddle a little slower, and glided onto the skin of the water. I ran to my father, took his hand, and didn't look back.

That's the third thing you should know.

And now we're finally *inside* the church, with its long polished pews, the chalice on a raised dais, tall windows that filter the light. Abbe and I find our way to a pew in the center, near the back, and sit on the aisle to facilitate an easy escape if necessary. I'm already regretting a little bringing her to church. She's such an excited and sociable dog; it's torture for her to be bound to her leash while so much activity swirls around her. I put her on my lap, but she won't stay there, and so I place her on the floor, where she practically flattens herself sideways to say hello to the Husky mix in the pew two rows back. The church is filled with roaming packs of kids in the aisles, *dogs in church!* Like heat-seeking missiles, they track down huggable dogs, and mine, of course tops the list. One boy, about ten, strolls down the aisle with a beatific smile, greeting the animals one by one, and when he bends down to pet Abbe he does so with such grown-up control and purity of intention that he seems much wiser than his ten-year-old countenance would seem to allow. He looks her in the eye, fondles her ears, and she sits for him, gazes adoringly into his face.

But the rest of the children, mostly gangs of girls in odd, mismatched outfits—red tights under a purple dress; paisley top with striped jeans—hoist Abbe clumsily in their arms, pummel her with many hands at once. And while Abbe doesn't seem to mind, in fact she loves it, I feel a pang of juvenile possessiveness—my dog! I want to say and snatch her back in my arms. But I let them maul her awhile before I gently extract her, saying *she's a little wiggly today, let's give her some room.*

There are many familiar faces here: a former student waves to me from the back row, her large dog sitting docilely at her feet. A colleague sits a few rows over, pictures of her cats clutched in her hand. Others look familiar but I can't place them precisely; it's a Bellingham phenomenon, where nearly everyone looks dimly familiar because you've seen them so often at the co-op, or at the independent movie theater, or walking in the waterfront park. For a while last year I garnered the energy to take some classes, mainly to meet new people, and wound up seeing the same five women wherever I went. At first I found it depressing, but now there's something a little reassuring about it—this small community of the known world.

The minister finally calls the assembly to order, or to whatever semblance of order can be achieved with dozens of dogs in church. He says that for many reasons they'll keep the service rolling right along today—no sermon, for instance, and one dog howls. Everyone laughs, including the minister, who punctuates the end of the howl with, "Exactly!" There's so much movement in the pews, so much noise, and no one really pays attention to the initial announcements:

the progress of the pledge drive for the capital campaign, a young woman soliciting donations for her upcoming service trip to Kenya. We stand for the lighting of the chalice, and a young woman next to me shares her hymnal for the first song. My hands are full with Abbe, and I don't know the melody, and I'm still a bit shy of singing in public ever since my grade-school quarrel with the Star-Spangled Banner—but I do know it feels good to be standing with an armload of dog amid this human and animal cacophony. So I hum.

Here's the last thing you should know:

When I brought Abbe home—the first dog I've owned in the forty years since Sheba died; a dog I knew was *my* dog just from a thumbnail photo on the Internet—my father was in the hospital. January 3, a Wednesday, and he'd been there since New Year's Eve, when a guest at their party said to him: *You don't look so hot.* They abandoned the homemade éclairs and took him to the emergency room, where he turned out to have a blood infection, and though no one uttered the word *septic*, I knew from watching too many medical dramas that's how it's described—the body now toxic.

So, while my father has antibiotics pumped into his veins, drugs that don't seem to work and then they do, I keep my gaze focused on this new creature in the house: eight pounds of fur and bone and eyes and heart, a creature who immediately takes to sliding full tilt across the linoleum, then standing stock-still in the middle of the kitchen floor, ears akimbo, tongue out, as if to ask what we're going to do next. A creature who sleeps fine all night in her crate, but who keeps me up anyway, just by her presence. A dog who never barks, who doesn't need to, because I'm looking at her every minute. My gaze is so full of dog that when I leave her for one hour to go to a yoga class, she appears as an after-image every time I close my eyes.

And when I call every day to the Chandler hospital to get a progress report on my father, we talk for a just a few moments about his physical condition; he either describes his body's insurrection with a little bit of a bemused chuckle, or he takes on the command of the engineer, explaining the mechanics of what happened with professional curiosity. And then we immediately slide into dog talk. My parents now own two dogs: one a stolid corgi mix—she seems to be mixed with border collie, which makes for a rather odd-looking thing—named Tessa, rescued from a shelter many years ago, and the other a hyper toy-poodle named Maggie, whom they took over from my little brother's family when she proved to be too much for them. Once all their kids left home—all those allergic kids—my parents reverted back to the dog people they'd always been, and they've had some form of dog in the house for over twenty years.

Halley, their cocker spaniel, lived a long time; he was a good-natured boy, his skin loose and easily massaged with a palm. When he died, my father called me. "I have some bad news," he said, then paused. In that pause, my heart stopped. "Halley's no longer with us," he said, and my heart started up again, beating too hard in my chest. My father's voice stuck in his throat; he could barely say anything more, just repeated *no longer with us* as he struggled not to cry. I had never heard him so raw, filled with a grief he was willing to share.

Now, as I talk long-distance to both my parents—as they sit together in the sterile light of the hospital and wait for my father's blood to come clean—we chat with an ease and camaraderie that has never been quite so available before. We deflect our gaze toward Abbe, this animal we can exclaim over and love together simply and fully, without complication—and in so doing, feel that love refracted back onto each other. We talk about all those things no one else could bear: poop and pee, kibble and bones, leashes and halters and little doggie raincoats I never thought I would buy. We talk about sibling rivalry (Madrona yowled and swatted the dog within five minutes of being home), and we talk about the more numinous things, the things that can't really be articulated: the feel of a dog's paw, how you can run your hand over the pads of her feet for close to an hour. The texture of her belly, and the weight of her as she falls asleep crooked in your arm exactly like a small, contented person. The smell of her fur, a little like pears.

We can talk about all these things, and so not have to talk about what might happen next for my father. We all like this system, and we perform our parts with gusto. But on Friday the news is not good: they checked my father's heart as a matter of routine and found four blockages, unrelated to the blood infection. The doctors recommend triple-bypass surgery, and soon. It's as if my father's body knew something was up and had to do something drastic to get his attention, put him in the hospital where he belonged.

Over the weekend, I worry about whether I should fly to Arizona and be there on Monday for the surgery. I have a new dog, work is busy this week, it's quite impractical, but what if? My mother says I don't have to come, my father says I don't have to come, but my brother says, in a mysterious tone: *Make your own choice.* I think about a trip I took with my parents to France last June: we roamed all over Paris, in a heat wave, and as always my pace was invariably quicker than theirs. I had vowed to be a good, compassionate, patient daughter on this trip, but sometimes I couldn't help it, I just strode ahead without them. All weekend, one image flashes obsessively in my mind: my father panting to keep up, sweat on his brow, a crepe in hand, asking me in a plaintive voice: *Can we slow down for just a minute?*

On Saturday I go to my yoga class and start crying during corpse pose; my body's never been one to pretend. Everyone keeps saying how easy heart bypass is these days, how they've got the procedure down to a quick mechanical fix, but I've never heard my father scared before, and now I hear him scared. He's questioning whether he should have the surgery at all; there are risks either way, he's a diabetic, anything can happen. He's upset that he won't have the chance to get his financial papers in order for my mother. He misses the dogs, Maggie and Tessa, and just wants to go home. We keep talking about Abbe, change the subject to puppy whenever we have the chance.

And the puppy just keeps being a puppy. Her tail seems to grow inches every day, and all my friends come by to get acquainted, each time exclaiming how wonderful she is, which in turn makes me feel as though *I'm* wonderful, and I know I'm idiotic with joy. It's an odd state: to be so filled with happiness and so beset by terror at the same time. To be in the middle. I comment to my Buddhist friends that perhaps this is what is meant by the Middle Way, and I'm only half joking, because even as I swerve between tears and laughter, I also feel wholly present—a sharp watchfulness lingers.

On Monday, the day of the surgery, I talk on the phone to my father in pre-op, and since the surgeon is running late, I also talk to my mother and two brothers and my sister-in-law, all of whom ask about the dog, and all of whom seem eager to talk about her, even through the strain in their voices. They ask how Madrona is faring with the new addition. They ask how housetraining is proceeding. I tell them of the baby teeth I find—odd, blood-specked pebbles on the floor. We speak of all the small matters because the big matters too much. And maybe because the moment seems so portentous, or maybe because there is another creature here to absorb our attention, all of them seem to love me a little more easily, to annul whatever hurt or distance there's been in the past.

My father, it turns out, will come through the surgery just fine, and even a day later will sound more healthy than he's been in years. He'll speak with more clarity, the oxygen flowing unimpeded through his heart. But right now we can't know this, we don't know what kind of future we face. So, for now, Abbe lies next to me on the couch, and I stroke her belly with my knuckles as I talk with my family, the cell phone passed from hand to hand in that far-away pre-op room, their voices muted but legible. I think carefully about what words to say to my father, because no words will be enough. The one word I don't want to say: goodbye. I touch the puckered scar from Abbe's spay, a small ridge that disrupts the expanse of her shaved, mauve underbelly. The dog, of course, is oblivious; she has no idea of herself as a lifeline. For her, it's just another day, another good day.

That's the last thing you should know.

And now Abbe and I, we're back in church; you can find us in the third pew from the rear, Abbe standing with her front paws on the back of the bench to get as good a view as possible. *Dogs in church! Dogs in church!* And now, it's time: the minister asks his assistants to move down the right and left sides of the aisles, while he descends from the altar and begins making his way up the center, hitching up his robes and kneeling as he arrives at each parishioner with a pet. I can't hear what he's saying—the noise level rose as soon as he descended, and by the way he leans close to each one I can tell this is a private moment, not meant to be shared. And the kids have taken this as another pet-every-dog-possible opportunity, darting up and down the aisles, but somehow maintaining a bubble of calm around the minister, veering away from him in convex patterns.

When I decided to come here today, I hadn't really thought about how the blessing, itself, would be administered—this one-to-one, head-to-head communion. I envisioned more of a parade of the species, with each of us leading our animal toward the altar, blessings dispensed like rain, falling on everyone at once. But this is better. I'm glad to be sitting on the center aisle, since a blessing from the priest is more likely to be potent.

As he draws near, I fumble with one hand in my purse for the picture of Madrona, while trying to get Abbe to lie still in my lap; she stretches out full length, making herself as long as possible, trying to get close to the floor where the dogs and children mingle. Even the adults in the congregation have caught the fever, and they, too, begin to roam a bit, greeting friends, leaning over the pews to talk. A few rows ahead of me a teenaged girl holds a tiny puppy wrapped in a blanket against her shoulder; the dog can't be more than 8 weeks old, too young to be here, I think, amid so much frenzy.

And then, here he is, the minister, looming above us, a tall man with a whiskered face, his red-and-white robes fluttering in the breeze generated by all the commotion in the aisle. He kneels and asks, *Who do we have here?*, and the din in the church recedes; it feels as though we've acquired a shield, something like the "dome of silence" that used to descend on Max Smart, the spy in my favorite television show as a kid. And I tell him this is Abbe, and she has a sister Madrona, holding out her picture. *Good,* he says, *we'll keep Madrona in our thoughts as we pray.*

And then he lays his right hand on Abbe's head, a head that has miraculously gone still, and now she just looks up at the minister with the same calm gaze she gave to the young boy, tongue at rest in her mouth, eyes half-closed as if in pleasure. He says to her, in a voice low and kind: *May you live a long life of love and peace,* and some other

words I can't quite catch because just then my eyes begin to fill—
I hadn't expected this—and I'm trying to concentrate, to say the
words silently with him, but it's difficult, because in this moment I
know how much I really do love this dog, and how this love breaks
me. It's as if the minister's reached in and laid his meaty palm right
on the muscle of my own heart—every animal part of me that longs
to feel blessed has risen to the surface, like koi in an algae-filled
pond. Sheba's there, and that daffy duck waddling toward me, and
my father's heart still pumping . . . *and may we pray in love, amen,* and
I croak out an *amen,* and a *thank you,* and then he's gone, and a pack
of children and worshippers rushes into the eddy he leaves behind.
A woman asks, cheerfully, *What kind of dog is this?,* oblivious to the
tears I'm wiping away with the flat of my hand.

I mumble an answer, feeling a little foolish that I'm so shaken, but
what can I say, there are *dogs in church!,* and I gather up Abbe and her
leash and her treats and we make our way toward the back of the
sanctuary, where everyone has circled up for the closing hymn. My
dog and I take a place at the end of the line, the circle here petering
out into a ragged spiral. I hold a stranger's hand with my right hand,
Abbe with the other; Madrona is folded up in my purse. I look around
the church to see—lined up along the walls, under the windows—
a hundred familiar faces gazing into the center, their voices giving
blessing to all that is animal, the animals blessing us in reply. I hoist
a panting Abbe onto my hip, and we sway in perfect time to a song I
have no idea how to sing.

A THOUSAND BUDDHAS

A Dharma Name

This morning I'm going to receive my dharma name. I kneel in the zendo, amid the bowls of oranges and the sticks of incense burning in neat piles of ash. Orchids adorn the Buddha, and a few sprigs of lily and thyme. Many candles burn through the early-morning dark, gilding everyone in the circle with a golden aura. Last night our teachers, Arnie and Therese, asked who might want to formally receive the Buddhist precepts; in doing so we'd be given a name in return: a dharma name, a private name, one that might reveal in its syllables a true self that until this time remained hidden.

It was the name that did it for me, an incentive like the gifts they offer on public radio pledge drives. How could I refuse? All my life, it seems, I've been searching for a name that embodies me without distortion. My brothers called me Ben, and I toddled through my childhood this truncated self, becoming what my brothers wanted me to be: diminished, easy to play with. I renamed myself Amanda when I was eight years old, lengthening myself into the undulations of three syllables. In college, I was Little Raven, trying to speak in the native phonetics of birds. In Hebrew school, I'd been *Basha Leah*, a girl in another language, a girl with whom I might correspond, writing in the strange alphabet of Judaism.

For this dharma name, we didn't have to take all five of the Buddhist precepts: only the ones we honestly felt we could keep. So last night, on a piece of scratch paper, I wrote out which vows I would take and why: the second precept, against stealing in favor of generosity; and the fourth precept, to speak the truth as clearly as one can. I feel a little wimpy: I took those two, really, because they seemed easier than the others, the only ones that required neither renunciation nor hardship. But the precepts are tricky; I know that to live my life in accord with even these two relatively simple vows will require a great deal of integrity, and perhaps even sacrifice.

All night I wondered what my new name might be, and I recalled the Buddhist appellations I know: True Seed; Vessel of Light; Perfect Knowledge. Thich Nhat Hanh, a Vietnamese monk, wrote a poem "Call Me By My True Names," and by this he means he is several, he is Whitman's multitudes. "Please call me by my true names," he writes, "so I can hear all my cries and laughter at once. . . ." In the poem he becomes the starving child in Uganda, and the arms merchant selling weapons to Ugandan military; he becomes the 12-year-old girl raped by pirates on a boat out of Cambodia, and he becomes the pirate who rapes her. By this roll call, he finds his true self revealed, an identity bound to that of all humanity.

In northern California, where I lived for many years, people changed their names quite frequently, shedding identities that seemed to bind them like ill-fitting clothes: there was Cypress and Enchanté, Nighteagle, and someone who called himself *Am*. Sarah, at fourteen, renamed herself Strawberry. Marybeth, a good Catholic girl from Boston, renamed herself Rhea Green, a woman who now found herself kneeling, revering the first shoots of the potato, the tendrils of sweet peas and beans. When her son first emerged from her, in that round shack on the hill, I held him when a name did not yet contain him; I held him in the lightness, in this brief abeyance before he became the boy he would always be: Sean.

When I lost my two children, I realized afterward I'd forgotten to name them. They left so quickly after all, and everyone said no, they weren't children really, just small aggregates of cells. I didn't know I was grieving for children then. In the mornings I listened to the California rain as it pinned me to the bed, the sound of it gentle and steady, and felt only mild alarm that I could not move, could not eat, could hardly speak. At four weeks, each egg was barely fertilized; if the expulsions had not been so violent the embryos might have passed through me without notice. But they grew big enough to hurt me, that must have meant something, I thought, as I listened to the endless rain. Lately I've imagined the two of them as brother and sister, a boy and a girl: I even dreamed about them once, twins named Ira and Isabelle.

This morning, I kneel in the pre-dawn, in a line with five others who have decided to vow something, perhaps quite a lot, to receive a true name that might redeem them. And the names of my children return to me: Ira and Isabelle, Ira-and-Isabelle, like a chant, a mantra that might spur me toward enlightenment. My own names echo in my ears, multiple and confusing. I'm an impostor here, among the incense and the oranges. Can I really ever open my mouth without telling a lie? Can I really give and give without a thought of return?

But Arnie and Therese call me forward. I shuffle toward them on my knees. On either side of the aisle my sangha watches as I receive my name on pink parchment: *Kind Speech of the Source*, scripted in ink, stamped with a red seal. A name that speaks of incorruptible origins, clear thought, a pure land in which every shard is rendered harmless. It's a name I want desperately to be true. And my friends there, in the candlelight, in the downturned gaze of the golden Buddha, seem to think it is so: they murmur and nod their heads in assent.

Music of the Spheres

I too am untranslatable,
I sound my barbaric yawp over the roofs of the world.

—WALT WHITMAN

It took a mathematician, Pythagoras, to divine the "music of the spheres," convinced the planets resonated against one another in their orbits to build whole octaves, an amicable chorus. He called this "Musica Mundana," a sound we mortals fail to hear because it actually remains so familiar, humming as the backdrop to our ordinary lives. He also heard what he called a "Musica Humana," the continuous pitch each human body emits, much like the planets, all of us resonating either in harmony or dissonance between the soul and the body in which it is quartered. If we sit long enough in meditation, we start to feel this kind of vibrato: our bodies as throngs of molecules with wide swathes of space between them. Of course we emit music. How can we help ourselves? We are whole arias, rising and falling and rising again.

Sometimes I think I hear it: this faint music of the spheres. For two weeks I have a room in a house I'm sharing with two other writers at the edge of Tomales Bay. I'm in the room they call the "South

Tower"—upstairs, with its own deck and rocking chair looking out over the pastoral lands below. Fog does not roll in but lingers, a constant presence in the mornings as I rise early, take my first sips of coffee, gaze out at the S-curve of tall grasses and the herd of placid cows. A climbing rose encircles my deck, and below me gardens of lavender and sage spread out alongside the grass; honeysuckle still improbably blooms in August. The smell in the air blends all these with the faint undertone of cow, the elusive motif of salt and wind.

I've brought my little meditation bell, but so far every sound seems a call to mindfulness: the hummingbirds swooping past my ear, the insistent ravens, the occasional lowing of a cow. So why, then, am I having so much trouble actually setting pen to paper, doing what we think of when we consider "writing"? I've come here with a project, one that has been on my mind for nearly a decade, and now it feels just that: weighing on me, heavy and cranky, old bones creaking as I try to rouse it into action. So I spend most of my time outside in the little rocking chair, staring at the cows who seem to have it made: no projects for them! The quiet presses in around us, me and the cows; it takes on heft and vibrates against my skin, reverberations of celestial music reaching me light years away.

One afternoon, just as the sun makes its debut appearance, some new noises arise: a whoop, a loud grunt, a yodeling akin to a monkey's cry. A toy piano clinks a spacey melody, stopping and starting and stopping again, followed by a frantic banging on the keys. The quail in the garden flush up with a great whoosh into the trees, and a responding "whoosh!" echoes from beyond the side fence. Listening hard, I can locate these new sounds as the neighbor boy; our caretaker, Pam, had forewarned us of this possible disruption. In her gentle voice she had told us that a young boy who is "mentally challenged" lives next door; he likes to emit loud animal sounds and play with his music box for hours on end. She asked us for our patience, apologetically shaking her head at what she knew would be an intrusion.

For two days I hear him in the afternoons, my body tense, my mind growling all manner of uncharitable thoughts. ("Don't they know we're trying to *write* here!" or "Of course I can't get any work done *now*! Might as well go eat something.") Each time I hear him, I spend a commensurate amount of time wishing for the quiet to return, so that I can doggedly beat my head against my project, poke it around some more on the page. In the meantime, I rehash all my preconceptions: ideas about how retreats *should* work, memories of how they have played out for me in the past. I keep wanting *this* place to be *those* places; I feel as though I'm impersonating a writer, going through the motions, a shawl around my shoulders, my pen thoughtfully poised in the air, but not moving across the page.

Then, one afternoon, the boy lets out a particularly loud whoop and series of hollers, a stunning imitation of a car alarm (he reminds me, actually, of the mockingbirds I came to know one winter on the Yucatan Peninsula: they perfectly mimicked the scrape of tent zippers and the whir of film advancing in cameras). It startles me so much I drop my pen. And for some reason this time, instead of grousing, I simply sit and listen. I listen for a long time, as the day progresses across the pasture: the sun is out and then disappears again; the cowhands arrive on their ATVs and start nudging the cows toward home. My neighbor boy does a mighty convincing elephant, and the snorts of a wild horse. Now it's the baaing of a sheep. These sounds, guttural, burst from deep inside his body—Whitman's "barbaric yawp," brazen and unrestrained. This voice resists translation into any language that would seek to contain it.

His music joins in offbeat harmony with the birds that abide in the background: a madrigal. And as I listen I find myself *here*, really here, at Mesa Refuge: not in the places of my past where writing has previously occurred.

My meditation teacher, Eileen Kiera, often makes the point in her dharma talks to listen, without judgment, to all the sounds of the outside world (this teaching is particularly pertinent to our sangha, since the dharma hall sits on one of the busiest streets in town; our mindfulness bells are often drowned out by trucks braking outside, motorcycles revving, people laughing and shouting as they emerge from the Tex-Mex restaurant next door). She gently reminds us, in a voice so soft sometimes it can be difficult to hear the dharma over the rumble of trucks, that every sound in an invitation into the present moment, into an acceptance of things as they are. This teaching always makes sense to us, and we nod, and for a few moments we welcome the roar of a truck with the same equanimity as we would welcome the song of a sparrow.

In the meditation hall at Mountain Lamp, our rural retreat center near my house, we meditate in a large yurt set in a clearing on the hillside. I always love sitting in here when it rains, listening to the patter of drops on the canvas roof. Once Eileen told a story about a monk tapping on the glass of a huge fish tank, despite admonishments from aquarium officials. *But I'm trying to get their attention!* he laughed, and kept right on doing it, tapping gently on the glass with his pointer finger. "The world is like this," Eileen said. "It's always tapping on the glass, hoping we'll turn its way."

Eileen's teaching comes back to me now as the boy's cries—and the music box he plays with such abandon—become an organic counterpoint to the constant theme of crow, the upsurge of quail, the crescendo of wind off the bluffs. Even the water in the estuary, sparkling far off below Inverness Ridge, now seems to radiate a musical arpeggio, as do the blackbirds that swoop in massive clusters above the pasture. The boy's song merges with all this—no, more than merges, but responds with it, *corresponds*. His hullabaloo belongs to Mesa: a psalm that arises for only this place, and this time.

The music of the spheres, I think now, must be more wonderfully cluttered than we ever imagined, replete with truck horns and a boy's ecstatic cries, crows cawing and the wind off a restless bay. I imagine the spheres whirling and creating a vacuum that sucks in all the sounds that make up the world: power mowers, boys on their bikes and the cat's meow as she begs to be let in, all these whirling like scarves in the wake of one sphere to another, one human to the next.

One of my housemates, Elisabeth, is a playwright. She told us last night that she always compiles a soundtrack for each of her characters before she can really begin to write. She'll spend hours doing this, picking and choosing the songs that will help her know her characters completely. As she writes, this soundtrack plays on her headphones, weaving a space for the character's lives to emerge on the page. She makes soundtracks, she says rather sheepishly, for her own life as well, the songs articulating in perfect measure the quality of her life story as it plays out for months at a time. She has cases and cases full of CDs that she plumbs for this endeavor, with everything from the soundtrack to Felicity to the Bach cello suites.

We all do this, of course, throughout our lives: we latch onto songs that become anthems. When I was thirteen, I stood at my bedroom window and howled "If" from Bread (*if a picture paints a thousand words, then why can't I paint youuuuuuu. . . .*), my voice wobbling into the universe and adding to the legion of lovelorn voices that still echo among the planets. At twenty-one, Fleetwood Mac's "Leather and Lace" articulated the wordless shame I felt in an abusive

relationship (*give to me your leather, take from me . . . my lace. . . .*).
I sang it in my car on my way to work at a bakery at 4 A.M., my head
resting against the cold window, my lower lip trembling, the stars
and planets above emitting a cold light, absorbing my song. When
we sing these songs at full volume, driving down the highway, or
with mop in hand, scrubbing the floors, we suddenly seem aligned
with the music of the spheres, the melodies that keep our bodies,
those recalcitrant machines, humming.

I want to ask Elisabeth to make such a soundtrack for me, one
that includes, in fact, our neighbor boy's player piano, the chain
saws down the valley, the ravens and the sparrows. She has told me
she would love to be a soundtrack designer for film, but I think a
better job, a more noble one, might be to make soundtracks for
people's lives, to help them articulate all that cannot be said in words
alone. It would be the most lovely kind of therapy, a cross between
counselor and psychic: I imagine Elisabeth and her client sitting
across from one another, touching or not, as the right music passes
between them.

Now I can hear my housemates in the kitchen below me; the
working day must be coming to an end. Their voices murmur low
and soft, so as not disturb me in my "aerie," as we've come to call it.
But I want to tell them now that the noises of the world, at this
moment, do not disturb but mingle to create the most fitting soundtrack to my work. Their voices merge with the sound of dishes, something being chopped, cupboard doors open and closed. The quail
rummage in the clear patches below, their song a worried "click-
click" in the throat.

Far out in the now empty pasture, one of the cowhands steers, at
top speed, his ATV across the grass, and from across that distance I
can hear what sounds like a song. Yes, he sings loudly over the sound

of his motor, some tune I can't quite catch: his voice bumps when he goes over the hillocks and smooths out as he glides along the dike. The music seems to spill from him naturally, as he zooms through a field from which all his charges, his responsibilities, have fled. He herds nothing at this moment, only the empty field that swirls a little around this voice that evaporates into the air.

Just as suddenly as he appeared he's gone again, and the field seems more empty for the lack of him. Fog drifts in to take his place, and even this vapor has a sound, ticking over the domestic bushes, whispering through my hair. The geese fly overhead as they do every day at this time. You can't always see the birds in the fog, but you know them from the calls they send through the mist. And though they're not calling for us, in fact have no notion of us at all, we feel somehow saved a little by their song.

How to Meditate

Day 1

On arrival, huddle in the Volkswagen with your friends and eat all the chocolate in the car. Chocolate chips, old Kit-Kats, the tag-end of a Hershey Bar—do not discriminate. Feel deprived, then light up your last Sherman, pass it around. Watch your fellow retreatants flow into the meditation hall. Note how elegant they look, even in sweatpants and black Wellingtons. You'll wonder where they get such nice sweatpants. You'll look down at your baggy jeans, your dim T-shirt and say, *I'm not dressed for this, let's go home.* Look beyond the meditation hall to the Navarro River, the cattails, the red-winged blackbirds. It will be raining, just a little.

Remember that you've forgotten dental floss. Take a deep drag off the cigarette and wonder what you're doing here. Take a close look at your companions in the car: your boyfriend Seth, who is so much older than you, and your friends John and Rhea. Remember how the four of you, just days earlier, had wound up tangled in a bed together, a soft bed with a down comforter, lazily stroking each other's limbs. Feel ashamed. Feel superior. Say, *Ready?*

A woman with bristled red hair leads you and Rhea to the women's dorm. There will be a deck overlooking a marsh where the blackbirds clack and whistle in the reeds. Glance at the other women who are folding their extra pairs of sweatpants, their Guatemalan sweaters. Sit on the cot and pat it with one hand. It will be hard, unyielding, to help you obey the precept against lying in "high, luxurious beds."

Scope out the meditation hall. Set up your pillow, your blankets, next to the woodstove near the back door. Figure this will be a prime spot—easy in, easy out—and smugly wonder why no one else has nabbed it. Realize your mistake when, during the first sitting period, heat blazes from the stove, frying the hair on your shins. Slide away a little, quietly as you can, and bump the knees of the woman next to you. Irritation rises from her like a wave. Start to apologize but choke yourself off mid-whisper.

Sit cross-legged on your pillow, your hands palm down on your knees. Breathe. Your teacher, who is from Burma, perches on a raised platform, his belly round, his knees hidden under his white robe. He speaks in a voice so deep it vibrates beneath your skin. He repeats the word: *equanimous, equanimous*. Invent a strange animal, an *Equanimous*, half-horse, half-dolphin, gliding through the murky sea of your unconscious. Feel where the breath enters and leaves your body just below the nostrils, like a fingertip tapping on your upper lip. Concentrate on this sensation. Within seconds find yourself thinking about Rhea's hand on your breast. Go back to your breath. Find yourself thinking about pancakes, eggs, bacon. Go back to your breath. Spend your first hour of meditation this way. They call it "monkey mind." Picture your brain swinging through the banana trees, its little hands clutching the vines. Go back to your breath.

Feel the pain begin in your knees, between your shoulder blades. Shift a little and feel the pain travel up your neck, down into your hips. Open your eyes halfway and surreptitiously glance at the meditators around you. They look perfectly still, their backs straight, their zafus round and plump. Look at your own flat pillow spilling from beneath your thighs.

You don't have the right equipment for this. You better leave now, before you're paralyzed.

Day 2

Read the rules again: No talking, no reading, no sex, no drugs, no eye contact. Vipassana, they say, is the art of looking deeply. Be unsure about how deeply you want to look. Read the schedule six times— 4:00 A.M.: waking bell, 4:30–5:00: chanting in the hall, 5:00–6:00: sitting, 6:00–7:00: breakfast, 7:00–9:00: sitting, 11:00: lunch, more sitting, nap time, more sitting, tea at 4:00, no dinner, Dharma talk at 7:00, more sitting. Add up the hours of meditation and come up with the number sixteen. Figure this must be a mistake and perform the calculations obsessively in your head, your own private mantra. You're already so hungry it's difficult to concentrate. Think longingly about the chocolate in the car, and hate yourself for not saving just a little.

Go to breakfast. Hold a simple white bowl in your two hands. Stand in line with your fellow retreatants and note the radiant colors of their shawls, their scarves, the blankets they have draped over their shoulders. Shuffle your way to the breakfast table. There will be large urns full of porridge. Take some. Take too much. Take a banana. Realize that your boyfriend Seth is opposite you at the table. Watch his hand as it chooses a pear, puts it back, takes an apple, puts it back. Feel a surge of love and annoyance. Out of the corner of your eye see a glint of Rhea's blond hair. See a flash of John's denim shirt. Feel grateful and angry at the same time.

Sit down at the long picnic table and begin to eat your food. Realize you need some honey and scan the table, spying it at the far end. How do you ask for it without speaking? You decide to get up and fetch it yourself, to avoid making an embarrassing faux pas. When you stand up your knees hit the table, knocking over your neighbor's teacup. Irritation rises from her like a wave.

Go back to your room and lie down. Fall asleep. Hear bells ringing in the distance. Know that you are supposed to be somewhere, then sit bolt upright and run to the meditation hall. Slow to a casual walk when you approach the doors. Stand and listen to the silence a minute. Listen to the breathing. Open the door which creaks on its hinges. Tiptoe to your seat, aware of everyone aware of you, of your every move. Settle in. Breathe. Fingertip. Nostril. Etc. Feel an overwhelming desire to run screaming from the meditation hall. Think about pizza. A cigarette. A beer. Feel your breath for one, maybe two seconds. Feel your neck slowly seizing up. Fantasize about yourself paralyzed. Imagine Seth and John and Rhea caring for you, running cool cloths across your forehead. Imagine the three of them kissing you all over your numb body, trying to restore feeling. Gasp when the bell rings. Hobble out of the meditation hall.

Go to lunch. Hold a simple white bowl in your two hands. Shuffle forward and ladle yourself miso soup, rice, some wilted bok choy. Take too much. Reach for the tamari. Notice Seth watching you from the opposite side of the table and dab it on sparingly. Sit down and eat slowly, slowly. Wonder if there's dessert.

Day 3

When you wake up, you might hear two women whispering in the bathroom. If so, take the opportunity to feel superior. Calculate how long it's been since you've last eaten. Sixteen hours. This seems impossible. Wonder why everything adds up to sixteen.

Drape a blanket over your head and walk outside, toward the meditation hall. Notice the red-winged blackbirds, the budding lilac, the silver cast to the sky. You'll think it's beautiful. You'll think you'll have to get up earlier at home from now on. Pause for a moment and notice your breath, like a fingertip tapping on your upper lip.

When you enter the hall the chanting has already started. Your teacher seems to chant the word *Betamite* over and over, with variations in pitch and speed. Wonder what *Betamite* is. Think of it as a breakfast spread, sweet and salty at the same time. Think about breakfast. Calculate the amount of porridge you will ladle into your bowl. Top it with honey and a pear. Breathe. Notice yourself breathing. Notice yourself noticing yourself breathing. Your neighbor tips over, asleep, and wakes up with a stifled cry. Feel sympathetic. Smile a sympathetic smile to yourself.

In the afternoon take a walk down by the river. You do not have Wellingtons, so your feet get wet and cold. Your hands are freezing. You miss your friends. You feel alone in a way that is foreign to you. Try to remember if you've ever been so completely alone in your life, and realize how surrounded you've always been, how supported. Remember how you laughed in bed with Seth and John and Rhea. Remember the release of it, how it felt not so much like sex, but like love multiplied ten-fold.

Wonder if you'll ever be able to speak again. Try it. Open your mouth. Feel a tiny bit of panic tremble beneath your upper arm. Feel hunger in your belly like a wild animal.

Day 4

Just when you think you have it down, just when you've noticed yourself noticing your breathing for unbroken seconds at a time, your teacher tells you everything will change from now on. Now you must become aware of the sensations on the surface of your skin. Now you must scan your body, *sweep* your attention from head to toe, noticing the sensations arise and pass away. Arise and pass away. *Equanimous.*

Start with the top of your head. Feel your skull like a dumb shield, hard and unyielding. Feel nothing, then feel a slight tingling, a tear-drop of sensation. Notice it. Move your attention like a scrim down the crown of your head, to the tips of your ears. Feel an overwhelming desire to run screaming from the meditation hall. Return to what you know. That fingertip. Settle in with the fingertip tapping on your upper lip. Feel competent. Feel sly.

Thirty minutes later open your eyes halfway and, without moving your head, try to see toward the men's side of the room. Move your gaze past young men with straight spines, men whose faces seem chiseled, calm, focused, unconcerned. Find among these men your boyfriend, Seth. See his furrowed brow, his downturned mouth, his clenched fists. See him trying so hard. Look past him for John. Try to find John anywhere in the room.

When you walk back to the dorm, see Rhea flossing her teeth on the deck. Stop behind a tree and watch her floss and floss, the movements of her hand so practiced, her teeth so white. Feel at a loss when she turns around and heads back inside, the deck now so empty.

At lunch, take the right amount of salad, half a baked yam, stir-fried snow peas with tofu. Hold your bowl in both hands as you find your seat at the picnic table. Sit in the same seat every day, though you could sit anywhere you like. Try to eat with chopsticks, the way the people in radiant scarves do. Drop bits of food all over the table. Try to brush them away, casually, with the back of your hand.

You've memorized fragments of the people around you: a hand, a wrist, a thigh. You know their shoes: Birkenstocks, rubber boots, thongs. You recognize their smells: rose water, underarms, unwashed wool. Feel at home in this. Then feel surrounded by bits of people disintegrating.

At night, you'll have trouble sleeping, though you're so tired you think you might go insane. Breathe in and out. *Equanimous. Equanimous.* Your teacher's voice is the only one you hear all day, and so you listen carefully to every word he says. At night, when you cannot sleep, briefly worry about brainwashing. Think of your brains heaped in a sink, rinsed repeatedly in cool water.

Day 5

At 5:00 A.M. you'll feel as though you're in a film. Drape your blanket over your head, clutch it closed at your throat, so you're cowled like a monk. Think of an appropriate soundtrack, something with gongs and birdsong. On your way to the meditation hall, you might see someone furtively smoking a cigarette. If so, feel superior. *Sweep* your attention from the top of your head to the bottoms of your toes. Make it to somewhere mid-torso before you begin craving kisses, wine, a cigarette.

After breakfast it's your turn for karma yoga, which means you have to wash the dishes. Stand at the sink with a man who, out of the corner of your eye, looks incredibly handsome, radiant. He moves efficiently through the kitchen, drying the dishes you hand him with a rough towel. Imagine the two of you communicating without words as you plunge simple white bowl after simple white bowl into the hot water. Imagine you are married to him, that you have a house in the country with two dogs and a meditation room. Imagine the children you will have together, their terrible beauty. Feel him close by your side. He hands back a bowl you haven't washed properly; a gob of gray porridge clings to the rim. Feel as though you want to die.

Walk to the meditation hall in the rain. Think, *equanimous, equanimous*. Feel the water evaporate from your skin as you *sweep* your attention from the top of your head to the bottoms of your toes. Think about Rhea's hand on your breast, Seth's mouth on your lips, John's lips on your thigh. Try not to feel like a harlot. Try to remember how *natural* it all seemed at the time. Calculate how many different relationships must be nurtured in this foursome. Come up with the number sixteen.

At the Dharma talk that evening, discover that you will now have periods of "strong sitting." Now you must not move a muscle, no matter how painful the sitting becomes. Practice "strong sitting" for a half hour before going to bed. As soon as you begin, feel an overwhelming urge to run screaming from the meditation hall. Feel a sharp pain radiate from your hip, your ankle. Resist the urge to move. Feel the tension in the room rise.

Then, inexplicably, feel your body relax. Feel the pain arise and pass away, arise and pass away, a continuous and fluid thing, impermanent. Begin to feel a glimmer of understanding. Begin to see your body in these terms, arising and passing away. Even the muscles.

Even the hard bones. Even the core of you. Begin to wonder if the body that melted under the touch of Rhea's hand is the same body that now arises and passes away. Feel a bewildered sorrow. Return to your breath. Wait for the bell to ring.

Day 6

In the night, when you're not sleeping, have a terrible dream. Feel your body dissolve, turn into nothing but air. Not even air. Jerk yourself back. Lie there gasping for breath. Resist the urge to wake up Rhea, to lie down next to her, to feel her impermanent skin against your own.

Day 7

Decide to ask your teacher about this experience. You will go up to him during the question/answer session after the Dharma talk. Spend all day worrying about this, about what exactly you will say, what words to use. Worry that your voice might sound harsh and ugly, like someone diseased.

Wait your turn. Kneel next to the stage, and know that Seth can see you, and Rhea. Try to look serene. John, you think, has stopped coming to the meditation hall, has decided to find enlightenment on his own. Bad boy. Envy him his initiative.

Move forward on your knees. Kneel before your teacher. His face is large, larger than your head. His eyes are kind but almost all pupil, and you feel yourself drawn into them, spiraling the way you did in your bed last night. So lean back a little, take a deep breath. His wife, next to him, smiles at you and you suddenly want to cry. Say, *I felt myself.* . . . Start again. Say, *I have so much fear.* . . .

He laughs. Fear is fear, he says, impermanent, passing away. He waves his hand in the air, and for a moment it seems to vanish in a flash of white. Thank him. Return to your place near the woodstove. Breathe. Feel the fingertip tapping on your upper lip.

In the last meditation period of the day, have another dream. Think of yourself pregnant, squatting behind a chair, giving birth to a baby girl. Feel yourself split open. Feel the beating of your heart, your blood.

Day 8

Breathe.
Arise.
Pass Away.

Day 9

Begin to dread the breaking of Noble Silence. Begin to appreciate how much of your life is taken up with small talk and inconsequential matters. Swear you will get up earlier when you get home, you will speak only when necessary, you will be an equanimous person, even if you never touch Rhea or John or Seth again. Work hard at your meditation, so hard you break out in a sweat during "strong sitting." In the afternoon, realize that Rhea has been sitting behind you all along. Wonder how you missed her there, all this time. Before going to your seat, watch the back of her head, the set of her small shoulders. See her as a body already dead. See the flesh passing away until only a skeleton remains. Wonder how you will live your life from now on.

Begin to lift your head and look at your fellow retreatants. Notice that everyone seems a little worn down, pale, sallow. Look forward to washing your sweatpants, sleeping in your own bed. Wonder if you will be alone in that bed. Memorize a speech you will give to Seth, John, and Rhea. Swear you will love them no matter what happens.

Eat a pear for breakfast. Some rice and tofu for lunch. Steal some floss from Rhea while she's in the shower. Stop in your tracks at the whistle of a blackbird. Whistle back, a small sound made of nothing but air.

Day 10

Break the Noble Silence. Feel the buzz in the room. Everyone's giddy. You've all just returned from a trip to a foreign land; you all have pictures to show, stories to tell. Even the strangers look familiar to you. Say, *Don't I know you?* to everyone you meet. Notice the subtle glow around everyone's cheekbones. Sit with Seth and John and Rhea at a round table on the deck. Hear the blackbirds yukking it up in the glade.

Well, Rhea says, holding John's hand to her heart. *We've decided to have a baby!* A baby. The words seem so loud, so rough-hewn, you have trouble getting them from your ear to your brain. Rhea's gaze slides across your face. John looks straight at you and grins. Seth puts a hand on your shoulder, and takes it away again.

Forget the speech you were going to give. Start to tell them about the night you dissolved in your bed, about your fear of becoming no one, but halfway through sputter to a stop. Try to feel your breath like a fingertip tapping on your upper lip. Feel confused. Feel an overwhelming urge to run screaming from the dining hall.

Walk a path through wet grass down to the Navarro river. Say good-bye to the blackbirds and their red shoulders. Think you will always remember this, and know that you won't. Feel yourself rising and passing away, there by the river. Look upstream and then down. Feel yourself like a boulder in the middle, worn by the rushing water. Hug yourself. Feel your hands strong against your upper arms, hold-ing yourself in place.

A Thousand Buddhas

My hand's the universe,
it can do anything.

—SHINKICHI TAKAHASHI

I

I could tell you I once received a massage from a blind person, but that would be a lie. I've never been touched by someone blind, but I can imagine what it would be like. She would read me like Braille, her fingertips hovering on the raised points of my flesh, then peel back the sheets of my skin, lay one finger on my quivering heart. We could beat like that, two hummingbirds, and become very still. Her hands might move across my abdomen, flick the scar below my belly button. My eyelids would flutter at her touch, and my skin dissolve into hot streams of tears.

I have never been touched by a blind person, but I have given whole massages with my eyes halfway closed, and the bodies I touched became something else. Their edges dissolved, and they spread out on the table—masses of flesh, all the borders gone. I touched them in tender places: under the cheekbones, between the toes, along the high arching curves of their feet. When I opened my eyes these people coalesced into something human, but I walked outside and slipped into the pool, feeling like a primordial fish, all my substance gone. I'd see them afterward, and they leaned toward me, their mouths open, but they hardly spoke. My arms opened and they fell against me; I held my hands on the middle of their backs, holding their hearts in place.

Sometimes they cried. I was too professional, then, to cry, knew that I had to keep some distance in order to make this relationship work. If I had cried, then we might have been lovers, and that would make it wrong somehow when they handed me the check for thirty dollars. Sometimes they pressed it into my hands and looked away, said *I can't even tell you*. I nudged them in the direction of the baths, and they went like obedient children, their naked bodies swaying under their towels as they shuffled across the old wooden bridge.

II

I have a picture from that time—of myself in the hot tub at Orr Hot Springs. At least, some people claim it is me, pointing out the slope of my breasts, the flare of my hips, the circumference of my thighs. Positive identification is impossible since the woman in the picture cradles her face in her hands.

Light streams through a low doorway into the gazebo, and this young woman leans her back against the deck. The sunlight zeroes into a circle on her belly. Jasmine bush and bamboo are reflected in the glass. The woman bends her head and covers her eyes as if she were about to weep. Steam rises in flurries and beads on the glass, obscuring detail and memory.

The woman is not weeping. She is scooping up the water from the tub and splashing it to her face. If this woman is me, she is mumbling some kind of grateful prayer, alchemizing the water into a potion that will heal.

It's easy to know what we're doing, once we're not doing it anymore.

III

Before I lived at Orr Hot Springs, I spent a summer baking bread for fifty children on a farm outside Willits. I didn't know I was in practice for becoming a massage therapist, but I knew I mended wounds buried deep inside me as I handled the huge mounds of dough. ("Talking things out" carves paths around and in-between the issues, but the body knows things the mind could never face.) The repetitive motions of my hands—the grasping and pushing, the bend of my waist, the slow ache in my shoulder—before long, I became automatic and blank. I kept my hands covered in flour and thought continually of food, of what is nourishing. I dreamed of my mouth always open and filled.

Children clustered around me, tugged at my apron, took little balls of dough and rolled them lightly between their teeth. The bread rose and came out of the oven, broke into tender crumbs, tasted good. I watched the children and gave them small lumps of dough to press. I touched their miniature shoulders and smiled, but said very little. At the midsummer dance, they braided flowers into my hair and held my hands, as if I were an old person convalescing from a long, wasting illness.

IV

Today I look at my hands. I remember the bodies I touched, the lives that came through them. I look at my hands sometimes and trace the edges of my fingers, like children do in kindergarten on newsprint with green tempera paint. Hands become what they have held; our hands shape themselves around what they hold most dear, or what has made an impression, or what we press on others.

My friend Dana once grabbed my hand off the stick shift as I drove through L.A. "These," he said, running a fingertip around my palm, "are healing hands."

I drove with my left hand on the wheel, while he examined every finger of my right. I swerved to avoid a dog.

"They're like a sculptor's hands," he said dreamily, dropping my hand and gripping his own.

Dana is a sculptor, with a propensity for twisted nude forms, estranged limbs, fingers in a bowl. Once, he left for Ecuador and painted all his walls, the appliances, even his books, a startling white; a "blank canvas" he said, for his friends to spill upon. And we did, troweling up purples and reds, oranges and blues, a cacophony of personalities rolling across his walls.

I pressed my hands in blue paint and hand-walked an awkward bridge above his couch.

V

What follows may, or may not, be true:

My ex-lover Jon stepped inside and closed the door, settled himself carefully on the edge of my massage table. "I just came to soak in the baths, decided to get a massage on the spur of the moment," he said. "I didn't know it was you."

We stared at each other. I don't know what he saw in my face—a barrier perhaps, a careful retreat—but in his face I saw a deep sorrow. My eyes involuntarily shifted into professional gear, scanning his body, making notes: a slump in the left shoulder, a grim tightness in the left arm and fist, chest slightly concave, breathing shallow.

In massage school, before we were lovers, Jon and I had been partners. The teacher insisted on partner rotation, but somehow Jon and I ended up together more times than not. We learned well on each other. We breathed freely; we allowed each other's hands to cup the muscles and slide so slowly down the length of connecting fibers and tissue; we allowed thumbs to probe deep into the knots. It was like a dance, the way our teacher said it always should be, an effortless give and take, back and forth, with the breath as well as the body. Communication—transcendent and absolute.

"Listen," Jon was saying. "I understand if you don't want to do this." His body leaned toward me, and my spine tipped forward in response. A massage room is a very close environment. Intimacy is immediate; truth prevails.

I glanced away from him and gazed at the far wall, at the painting of *A Thousand Buddhas* Jon had given me as a graduation present. For the last year, I had looked at that picture every day, and every day it reminded me of Jon less and less. A process of pain, moving ahead on its own momentum. The primary Buddha sat in the center, immovable, surrounded by a helix of Buddhas that spun around and around.

My palms relaxed, a good sign. "It might be awkward," I said, "but I'll try." I took a deep breath and whatever had been prickling at my throat subsided.

What did my body feel when I placed my hands on Jon's back? My palms curved instinctively to the crook of his shoulders; my own shoulders softened and I asked Jon to breathe, and he did, and I inhaled with him, stretching my lungs, and on the exhale my hands slid down his back, kneading the muscles on the downward slide, pulling up along the lats, crossing over his spine, and again, and

again, until he seemed to flatten, and there was no distinction between the flesh of his back or the bones in his arms or the curve of
his buttocks—no distinction in fact between his breath and mine. I
felt a small opening in my heart, a valve releasing, and an old love, a
love aged and smooth as wine, flowed down my arms and onto Jon's
skin. I knew, then, that sometime in the night I would remember this
gushing, and I would be shattered by a sense of tremendous loss, a
grasping ache in my palms, and I would cry, but even this certainty
could not stop my hands in their circular route through Jon's familiar
and beautiful body. He inhaled and began to sob. The tears shud-
dered through his back, his arms, his legs, and I felt them empty from
him in one bountiful wave. My right hand floated to rest on his
sacrum. My left hand brushed the air above his head in long, sweeping arcs.

There is a powder that covers the heart, a sifting of particles fine
as talc. It is protection—gauzy and insubstantial, but protection
nonetheless. Occasionally, a hand rubs against you and wipes a patch
clear.

That's when the heart bulges, beating with a raw and healthy
ferocity.

VI

There is another picture, one that is hidden in a drawer. It is me,
before I moved to Orr Springs; me, before I even knew such places
existed. I am young, young, young.

I am standing barefoot on the porch of a forest service cabin in
Prairie Creek State Park on the north coast of California. It is late
summer. I am wearing a purple tank top, tight Levis, and a forest
ranger's hat. The morning sun is full in my face, and I am smiling a

goofy, lopsided grin, my hands at my sides, my feet planted solidly on the wooden planks.

In this picture, I'm pregnant.

The pregnancy will end one week later, but in the picture I don't know this. I don't even know I am pregnant. I'm twenty years old and healthy from a long summer in Wyoming. It is a beautiful morning, and I am happy to be back in California. My world has not yet shifted to include the indifferent hands of nurses, the blind lights of an operating dome, the smell of bandages steeped in antiseptics and blood.

Look carefully at the belly for some sign of the child, at the face for some indication of motherhood. There is none; the snapshot is flat and ordinary: a young woman on vacation, nothing more. But I look at this photo and sense a swelling in my pelvis, a fullness in my breasts. I feel my skin inviolate and smooth, the substance of everything I've lost and meant to regain.

VII

Someone called them midwife's hands. A midwife's hands cradle and protect, hold a life between them. The classic posture for the hands in photographs you see: one hand cupped under the baby's emerging head, the other lightly curled on the baby's crown.

There is a polarity position like this: at the client's head, cradling, not pulling but imparting the sense of emergence just the same. If you stay long enough, motionless, the head appears to become larger; it grows and trembles. Sometimes I have touched the top of my head to the top of my client's head, and we are plugged in; we take big breaths, heave long, important sighs.

VIII

Sean was born. Not from my body. From Rhea's. I held the mirror at an angle so she could see the crown of his head as it split her body in two.

The midwife placed one hand on the skull and rotated it so the face pointed toward heaven. The eyes were open, glazed with an unearthly shine.

Rhea screamed. The world paused and listened. The body followed, sheathed in cream and wax.

IX

What does the body hold? And how do the hands release it? In the late seventies, "hug clinics" opened on college campuses in California. Distraught people were invited to drop in if they needed to be held in place by a pair of strong, encircling arms.

One of the most powerful massage holds I've used has the client on his side, curled into a fetal position. I cupped one hand to the base of the spine, the other lay flat on the back between the shoulder blades. These are the two places our mothers' hands fell when holding us as babies.

Some people cried with little shoulder-shaking sobs. Others fell promptly asleep. Most of them believed my hands were still on them long after I'd walked away.

X

In the hospital, the nurse stuck an i.v. needle into the back of my hand, over and over. I squinted and clenched my teeth.

"Does that hurt?" the nurse said, looking up, scowling.

I nodded.

"It's not supposed to hurt," she said, and set the needle aside, tried again.

When she was done, I lay on top of the covers, shivering, my eyes halfway closed, my palm flat on the bed. The i.v. fluid ticked into my blood. Already, I could feel myself forgetting everything.

My body was a container of pain. And then it contained nothing. An absence so absolute I couldn't even cry.

XI

The hand is shaped to touch the different parts of the world. We hurt, and the hand reaches to the chest. A newborn's head fits snugly into the center of a palm. Fertile soil runs through our fingers, or we mold our hands into a cup sealed for a drink of water. We can use our hands like primeval jaws to pluck whatever is ripe.

The midwife had fingers so long I almost asked her if she played the piano. The words were nearly out of my mouth, but then she handed Sean to me, and I forgot about pianos, about that kind of music.

I held him while the midwife and Rhea struggled with the afterbirth. I held him against my shoulder. His eyes were open; he blinked slowly and rarely, like a baby owl. The light in the room was gold, the color of honey.

I thought I saw something in his eyes, but I can't be sure. I thought I saw a nod of acceptance, a little man bowing to me, his hands pressed together in an attitude of prayer.

XII

They came to me hot and pink from the baths, most of my work already done. They came naked and slick and gorgeous.

What did I give them? Nothing but myself, and not even that, but the benefit of my whole attention, the focus of my hands on them, the focus of my heart. I don't know how long the change lasted. They left the room and lingered in the baths, got out, got dressed, and drove the two-and-a-half hours home. I waved good-bye and walked up the steps to my cabin, looked out my window to the woods, and thought about these people more than I probably should have. When the time approached for me to leave Orr Springs, I thought about them with a frantic longing for a life that could be balanced and whole.

I wanted to massage myself before I left; I wanted to send myself off with a stroke of my fingers, a hand along my spine, an affirmation for abundance, a momentary release from every memory that weighed me down. I thought it might help, if only for the drive out on the rutted and dusty road.

XIII

Years after I left Orr Springs, I worked for the Human Resource Council in Missoula, Montana. I didn't massage people anymore. I tried, but I zipped through the parts of the body as if I were taking inventory. I chattered like a barber giving a haircut. I thought about dinner, gas mileage, bills to be paid.

In my job, I interviewed clients and determined their eligibility for a heating assistance program. Many of the people I saw were elderly and disabled; all of them had stories to tell, stories that could take a lifetime. I had only twenty minutes to spend with each one.

I found that when I gave them my whole and complete attention for even five minutes, that was enough. I looked them in the eyes and smiled, laughed with them, murmured consolations. They looked back and told me what they knew. My hands kept very still on my desk.

One 76-year-old woman spoke to me in short, disjointed sentences, her head nodding emphatically with each word, spittle forming at the corners of her mouth. She smelled of cigarettes and bitter lemons. As I walked her to the door of my office, she swirled around and grabbed me by the waist. I settled my arms onto her shoulders. We stood like that for a few seconds under the fluorescent lights, the computers humming around us. I slid one hand down her back and held her there; my hand quivered, near as it was to her old and fragile heart.

XIV

I'm lying on my massage table. It's for sale. I'm lying on it, and I feel utterly relaxed. My breath swirls through my body in a contented daze.

I'm lying on my back. I open my eyes, and I see my face. I see me leaning over the table. My right hand comes to rest on my womb; my left hand hovers over my throat.

Forgive Me. Those are the words that pass between us.

Twelve Ways of Looking at Patience

I learn it every day of my life, learn it with pain I am grateful for:
patience is everything!

—RAINIER MARIE RILKE

Patience *n. A minor form of despair, disguised as a virtue.*

—AMBROSE BIERCE

I

Be patient, my mother says, and this admonition has the opposite
effect; instead of the calm she hopes will subdue my twitchy body, I
feel instead only a rise of agitation, of desire. I look away from her
and at all the temptations in my line of vision: predominantly candy
(the Mounds bar, the Three Musketeers, rustling packets of M & M's),
and trinkets (nail clippers, dental floss, a tiny flashlight the size of my
thumb). And next to that—oh cruel world, with all your lures—the
Pez candy dispenser with a Bugs Bunny head. Oh, how I want. I want
and want and want.

The checkout aisle smells of bubblegum, cardboard, and money.
There's the music of the cash registers, a bit like the sound of the

typewriter my mother commands at home, only slower, more deliberate, each number punched with deliberation. The murmur of women
talking or, even louder, the sound of them *not* talking—just emana-
tions of boredom, or anxiety, or the wish to be home in front of the
television, watching the soaps. They lean on their carts, soft arms
crossed on the handle, the afternoon too heavy to be borne by the
body alone.

My mother and I: we know each of these aisles of Hughes Market
by heart. Today, my mother is pregnant with my baby brother, but I
don't know that yet. We both know she is tired, moving a little more
slowly than usual with her three-year-old daughter in tow. She con-
sults her list to make sure she remembered every item carved onto it
in her meticulous handwriting.

And me: I want and want and want. I want both the tiny flashlight and the Pez with a passion that scares me, a desire I can't really
understand. But what I do understand, quite clearly: I can't have
both. I may not get even one, but both—that would be impossible.
A miracle.

I'm up against my mother's leg, clad in its sheath of beige polyes-
ter; behind me another cart muscles into the line, the grill of it glow-
ering a bit too close. The woman in charge of this cart plucks one of
the magazines from the rack, flips the pages quickly, and drops it in
her cart. Just like that. She wants it, she can have it—a proximity
between desire and fulfillment of desire that leaves me a little dizzy.
She leans on her cart, glances down at me where I'm staring. She
gives me a quick half smile, close-mouthed, and turns away; her gaze
meanders over the heads of other shoppers, comes to rest on the
automatic doors that whoosh open and closed—it's gotten busier just
in the last few minutes, school must have let out, and now I hear
other kids in the checkout lines, whining for candy, for toys.

I am not a whiner, not yet. I wrap an arm around my mother's leg and sway against her; she looks down for a second, smiles, puts her hand on my head, but looks up again quickly, back to where she is watching the girl ring up her purchases, keeping tabs to make sure there are no mistakes because mistakes *do* happen, her fan of coupons at the ready. The girl takes each item in hand, turns it over for the price, punches it into the register with her manicured hands.

I take a chance, make the agonizing choice: the Pez. Pez, with its cunning little dispenser, the way each candy will appear as if by magic on Bugs Bunny's tongue. Never knowing you're at the end until nothing arrives.

I hold it up. I say, quietly, Mommy, *please?* She looks down again, and in that one moment I see her choosing between exasperation and pleasure. She likes Pez too, this I know. I know she likes the way a treat arrives out of nowhere. Who wouldn't? Who wouldn't love to see it again and again—that little rectangular tab of condensed sugar, clicked into place, offered again and again.

Her purchases pile up at the end of the conveyer belt, where a boy slips them in the stiff bag with expertise, knowing just where to put the cans of green beans, the frozen corn, the milk. He has one arm in the sack as a guide, and with the other hand he tosses cans and jars to nestle perfectly in place. Usually I love to watch him at this task he has perfected, a skill that must have taken a great deal of patience to learn. When I grow up I want to be a bagger, to fill sacks with lightning precision. But I know I must keep my eyes on my mother at this crucial juncture.

Okay, she says, and pleasure blooms in me: not only at this granting of my wish, but at the knowledge I made the right choice. She never would have said yes to the flashlight, this I know now with certainty. But then she takes the package from me, places it on the belt, which is quickly becoming empty of things to buy. *But be patient,* she says, *we'll open this when we get home,* and just as quickly as it became mine, the Pez is gone, up there in the realm of everything that comes to those who wait.

II

Patience implies waiting, but *being* patient is actually quite different from waiting. Waiting implies an end to the waiting; you are waiting *for.* While patience has no destination, no object for the sentence. It is a state of being without end. It does not necessarily obey the agreed-upon strictures of time.

The source of all our pain, my meditation teacher once said, is being in a hurry. *Im*patience: say the word and you feel it: that agitation in the chest, a tension that leads all the way up into the neck, the hands. It makes you want to hit something. Impatience implies an obstacle, something that gets in the way.

But Patience. Patience is the woman I see every other day walking with an elderly woman to the rose garden next to my house. They don't seem to be related (they both seems too cheerful for that); they walk arm-in-arm, inching across the street, slow step by slow step, the younger woman smiling as she matches her steps to the elder, talking, talking, talking while the old woman inclines her head. They don't walk far. Just to the bench in the center of the rose garden where they sit, and then I lose interest, never see them when they have chosen to rise and leave for home.

> *If you are wholly perplexed and in straits,*
> *have patience, for patience is the key to joy.*
>
> —RUMI

The command *Be patient* is usually said with Impatience. Even to ourselves. And thus all our contradictions are born.

III

There exists a clear etymologic link between patience and the noun "patient," one who comes to doctor for a cure. To be a patient is to hold the "quality of being patient in suffering." To be patient originally means to endure pain. And to do so stoically, not pestering the doc with information you've gleaned from the Internet, or from those commercials you see on television at 2:00 in the afternoon or 2:00 in the morning—the two poles of the day when suffering becomes most apparent.

Curing takes patience. Whether curing the body, the mind, or olives, or meats. They all take time. To cure implies taking care, making whole, softening. The word "accurate" stems from the word "cure," so when we move toward a cure, we are moving toward accuracy—toward pinpointing what is most precise, most true. Curing brings out the truth of a thing.

Truth is patient. It can wait all day.

IV

You need to practice restraint sometimes, not to eat the entire sleeve of Pez all at once. One at a time, the tablets pop out, and you take them gingerly onto your tongue.

Pez dispensers were originally designed to look and feel like cigarette lighters, intended to give the same brand of satisfaction: click and something is dispensed, whether it be sugar or flame. The cigarette lighter fits handily into a palm, and that was part of the appeal of Pez dispensers, the way they conformed so easily to one's hand, could be something to grip, something that measured time in sugar-coated increments.

I used to be a smoker. I would sit outside on various porches, on balconies, on lawns, pull out a Marlboro 100 and place it between my lips. I would get out the Bic lighter and click it once then twice (it never lit on the first try). I loved everything about smoking: the smell of a new pack, the heft of the square box and the way the weight of it made such a slight, but noticeable, difference in my purse. I loved the sizzle of the flame on the paper, the way it ignited then caught the tobacco in a fragrant, acrid burst.

A cigarette measured time: the time of a coffee break, the interlude between appointments, the ellipses between thoughts. Cigarettes were my form of meditation before I knew what meditation could be: the focus on the breath, the simmering down, the patience to stay with that space in between the past and the future. Smoke made patience palpable.

It began early, age 16. I used to steal cigarettes out of my mother's purse, which always sat in the same place on the kitchen counter— my mother somewhere else in the house, vacuuming perhaps, and through this sound I could keep track of her progress. I slid two Benson and Hedges 100's from the case where she kept them, a leather clutch with a little clasp on it like a change purse. I stole the matches too, and since my mother wasn't supposed to be smoking either, I knew she couldn't bust me. I figured she wouldn't even notice anyway, not realizing how surreptitious smokers always keep close tabs on their stash, know exactly how many cigarettes are left in a pack, ration them out over the course of a day or a week.

I wonder now if she opened that case with its satisfying little click and noticed right away the empty space where those two filtered babies would have been, jostled the case a little and counted, sighed, thought of her daughter stealing them away back to her room, or to her car—a beat-up Pinto, green with white stripes—and it's not the cigarettes she minds so much as that empty space that says something has been breached between them. She might have thought about that little girl who accompanied her to the grocery store, who at least used to *ask*, who surrendered the desired thing into her mother's hand.

And now here she is, a mother of teenagers, with one son so angry he bangs his head against the wall, a daughter so withdrawn she hardly says anything at all, just skulks down the hallway to her room where she does god knows what, and then there's her youngest, a boy so good-natured and likable he is easily overlooked. *What's not to like?* she says of him frequently, and it's true: this youngest boy who simply watches his older brother and sister, quietly baffled at how they seemed to make their lives so hard. He hums to himself and paints murals and learns how to search for gold, holding that perforated pan over the little creek in the desert, sifting, sifting, sifting through the dirt.

But it's not really gold he's after. He loves simply squatting on his heels in an oasis, water trickling through the scrub pine, the smell of resin in the air. He shakes with infinite patience that pan, knowing by instinct the way silt eventually sloughs off to reveal anything that might shine.

> *Patience is not passive; on the contrary, it is active;*
> *it is concentrated strength.*
>
> ——EDWARD BULWER-LYTTON

V

Patience is a card game, the British form of Solitaire.

My mother played a lot of Solitaire; I would see her at the kitchen table, the cards laid out in the Klondike cross, and the rhythmic swoosh of her shuffle, the tap of each card on the pile, lulled me into a state of soporific calm. I could watch her play for a long time, and she would sometimes let me lean on her shoulder, eager to point out the black five on the red six, or snatching up the Ace of Hearts when it appeared on top of a rapidly diminishing stack. It must have taken all the fun out of it for her, but she let me do it anyway, because she was a mother, and mothers, as they say, must have the "patience of saints."

I am not a mother, and so I'm a little rusty in the art of saintly patience. I now play a lot of solitaire, a single person's game, and I don't like anyone kibitzing. Still, I often play this game in the midst of other people. During a holiday meal, say, or a party, I might seek out a battered deck of cards, shuffle them with my awkward, completely unprofessional shuffle (the old cut-in-half-and-wedge-them-together in some semblance of mixing up, one card always flying off, getting bent . . .), and begin laying down either a Klondike or Accordion game. I don't mean to be rude; for me this strategy to survive a party is the opposite of rudeness, for while I'm arranging the cards—taking satisfaction in the thwap, thwap, thwap of each one—I'm actually quite attentive to the hubbub around me, and I'll even chime in. But my eyes keep perusing the little stacks, looking for any connection I might have missed. I keep tabs on the little stacks of cards that remain hidden, that tantalizing unknown beneath the already known. Always, the possibility of winning. And always, the opportunity to cheat.

But that's where patience comes in to the game of Patience. You have to wait to see what will be revealed. You have to wait for that flush of joy that comes when the hearts—and all the rest of them—start to align.

The party goes on around me. People with drinks in their hands, or little plates of food. Idle gossip, chit-chat. Usually at such gatherings I'm ready to go home after the first hour, not patient enough to let a party slowly find its rhythm, reveal its hidden connections, the possibilities of friendship. But with the cards to occupy my hands, I'm able to keep half my mind occupied—the half that worries, the half that gets twitchy, the half that wants and wants and wants. *Be patient*, but I can't, I want to jump out of my own skin.

I am my own game of Solitaire, one that goes on a long time, with no end in sight. The cards keep coming, each one shifting just enough to give me hope: Here's the jack that matches the queen; here's the five that will open up that pile of clubs. At some point you have to consider the possibility you're not playing with a full deck. There might be a crucial card missing.

VI

Sometimes we say: "My patience is wearing *thin*." As if patience were a garment. A garment that gets rubbed too long in one place, needs darning, gets stretched out of shape.

I must walk slowly to match my step to my mother's now. I stop and zip up her jacket to the chin because her shoulder gives her so much pain. She is recuperating from both back surgery and shoulder surgery. Recuperation takes a great deal of patience, the opposite of the frustration that I see rise in her as she tries to do the dishes, sweep the floor. *It is what it is*, she says, often, but it's said with a sigh. That sigh reveals all. I see it in her face: the wearing thin of patience. As if patience were a cloak covering the wounded parts. A bandage that curls up at the edges, the adhesive tiring.

I falter, often. I snap at her. Speak condescendingly. Answer in one word. I am the opposite of patience. I am certainly not a saint, don't even live in that neighborhood, will never have a saint's zip code.

> *Who ever is out of patience is out of possession of their soul.*
>
> —SIR FRANCIS BACON

VII

I see a financial planner now. She insists my life expectancy is 105, a number that both astounds and terrifies me. It means I have to save money. A *lot* of money. I've told her that if I'm alive at 95 (the age where her diabolical little graphs show my money plummeting into nothingness), just shoot me. *I'll be long gone by then*, she laughs, though she can't be much older than me. She wears lots of heavy jewelry, belted suits; she always looks armored in money.

It takes a lot of patience, she says. Patience is at the heart of a comfortable future. Impatience is what's gotten the whole country in trouble, wanting what we want and wanting it now. Bolting at the first sign of trouble.

I was about to say I can't imagine myself at 104, the year before I'm supposed to die, but unfortunately I can imagine it quite well. I'm already in the nascent stages after all: lower back aching when I wake, the mincing steps I need to take to the bathroom. I try to remember what it feels like to *bound* out of bed, to have the body at the ready, but I can't. Sooner than I think, I'll be old, just like that. I'll want someone to match her steps to my own, to zip my jacket for me, to kiss me on the forehead as if I were a child she loves.

VIII

My mother spent the afternoons ironing, vacuuming, polishing with Pledge. She spent the afternoons drifting from room to room with clean underwear, socks. The houseplants accepted her watering. She sipped many cups of coffee. Shopping was a break as well as a chore. It must take a great deal of patience to be a housewife, to stay strong in your routines, to be a home maker, since home can be disrupted by the very children you seek to protect.

I wouldn't know. I am not a wife, and my house is not married to me. There are no children to disturb it: My house has its own rhythm of patience, a life that can feel quite independent of my own. Quiet pulses just before dawn. I wish I could stay there, sometimes, in that middle layer between sleep and waking. Like slipping between a sheet and a blanket.

Remodeling a house takes patience. Weather delays. Permitting delays. Materials delays. Coordination delays. Delayed gratification, the results put off. During the remodel of my dining room, I hummed to myself. I did crossword puzzles, jigsaw puzzles, shopped online for dining tables and chairs.

But in a way I welcomed it: this enforced patience. The sense that everything was still possible. Now I'm looking at planting shade trees to shelter the new deck, but trees take patience, take years to give you what you think you need, and by then, who knows? You might be a different person altogether.

IX

Loneliness is patience thwarted. The solitary person wades through loneliness—palpable as a water—to get to the other side. No that's not quite it: you don't know if there will be another side. Patience is not waiting for something to change. Nor is it a purposeful stroke toward solid footing, a destination.

Annie Dillard: ". . . the silence gathered and struck me. It bashed me broadside from the heavens above me like yard goods; ten acres of fallen, invisible sky choked the fields. The pastures on either side of the road turned green in a surrealistic fashion, monstrous, impeccable, as if they were holding their breaths. The roosters stopped. All the things of the world . . . were stricken and self-conscious. . . . There was only silence."

Dillard is describing loneliness, but a kind of loneliness that goes far beyond feeling lonely. It's the *self*-consciousness that gets you: your self suddenly big and awkward and out of place in the universe. The trick is not to run. The trick is to wait it out.

It never used to be this way. When I was a kid I played alone a lot of the time. Instead of loneliness, I remember a kind of relief to be with only myself, with no one to tease me or tell me what to do. I stomped in the deep puddles in my backyard after a heavy rain, creating small boats out of twigs and leaves. I sat in my room with my "Brenda the Nurse" doll, or I lay on my belly with the catalogue I'd ordered from American Airlines that displayed all the wonderful stewardess accessories you could buy (berets! sashes! little pins with wings!). Or sometimes I just sat on my bed reading until it grew dark. And sometimes I sat there just *thinking*. Thinking about what, I don't know. Sometimes I'd fiddle with a Pez dispenser even when it was out of Pez. I'd click and click and click.

Naturally my mother appeared periodically and said, *go find someone to play with*, and I would dutifully set down the catalogue or the doll or the book and wander outside, where inevitably a few other kids would show up and we'd get a game of hide and seek going, or drift through the neighborhood on our Schwinns, go to the 7-11 for Slurpees. But always I longed to be back in my room, by myself.

As a young woman, too, I spent days and days alone. I thought nothing of packing my knapsack and hiking alone for a long weekend around Mt. Rainier. I camped by myself in the Grand Canyon. I once spent four days alone on the shores of Lake Powell, in a place accessible only by boat, with just a tent and a few watermelons and a notebook. I must have fancied it a kind of vision quest; I remember the winds picking up and battering my flimsy tent, the preternatural calm when they ceased, and then lying on a rock and watching one raven fly overhead in a criss-cross pattern for hours, as if it had been sent to watch over me.

In places like that, you are not only patient, you *become* patience. Your thoughts syncopate to the respiration of the earth. You are not out of place, but *in* place—an in-patient in the waiting room of the world.

X

I used to be a massage therapist, back when my body was young and could stand being in the vicinity of so many naked bodies. When you are giving a massage, you must be patience incarnate. You must become quiet, kneeling or standing or sitting, practicing strokes and holds and stretches you've done a thousand times, but each time it must be new, each time the first time. This is what patience gives you. Patience + hands = healing: a particular and precise equation.

Patience measures your heartbeat, your pulse. They don't quit until they do.

Patience is a girl's name I adored. I wanted that name. A girl named Patience would always be beautiful. A girl named Patience would beam with kindness. Patience + time = compassion. Another sum, another scribble on the chalkboard before it's erased.

XI

Patience = prayer. Or prayer = patience. *Give me strength*, my father used to mutter to himself whenever one of us kids tried his patience. I don't know if his prayer worked, if strength infused his body and soul at that moment, but I know just the incantation gave him a moment, a space in between.

Patience does not require answers. Patience is merely the question asked.

Be patient toward all that is unsolved in your heart and try to love the questions themselves. . . . Do not now seek the answers, which cannot be given you because you would not be able to live them.

My old friend Rilke. He tried to be a patient man. His mother dressed him in girl's clothing until he turned five; she called him Sophia. She made him into a surrogate for his dead sister. Her grief could not be patient, could not allow her son to be her son. He grew into a melancholic man, a poet who tried to stay with objects long enough to divine the "silence of their concentrated reality."

XII

Patience is the dharma discussions we hold in our meditation group every month. Put your hands in prayer position, bow to indicate you're ready to speak. You speak without interruption, bow to sign off. Sit quietly for at least three breaths before indicating your own wish to speak. Those three breaths can take a long time, and you have to quell your desire to jump in, to answer any question that has been asked. The question must sit, settle, expand.

Because, it turns out, in dharma discussion it isn't so much what anyone *says*. Those three beats are really the most important communication of all—the silence in which we breathe, connected, wanting for nothing. Just listen: even when the words disappear into thin air.

Infant Ward

This child is not my own, but still the words of possession slip from me: *my baby girl, my sweet baby.* I've never seen her before this minute, but I think I know what she needs: the lights at her hospital bedside dimmed, her loose arms girdled securely against her chest. This patient has no name except "Girl _____," a family surname typed on the identification card at the end of her crib. She's too young, too early, to have a name like Betty, or Jennifer, or Anastasia. She surprised everyone, caught her parents without a crib or a car seat, without the casseroles in the freezer, without the stamina. I pat her back, I shade her eyes, I clutch both her hands in my palm, strong against her sternum. She relaxes and makes a sound—not a laugh or a sob, but something in between—a sigh moist with resignation.

It's a moment of simple communication, common here on the infant ward at Children's Hospital. I gurgle back to her and so we converse, our rudimentary voices vibrating the cord that governs reflex. Conflict resolution is reduced to this: she sticks out her tongue; I stick out mine. She blinks; I blink. She makes a gurgled moan, and so do I. She cries, and my voice veers up in commiseration: *Yes, I know, everything's going to be all right.*

Though, of course, I know no such thing. I know nothing about her except her immediate physical needs and desires. I don't know which organs are failing, or if there are gaps that weaken her heart, or where her parents might be. I'm just a volunteer; every Wednesday I put on a blue jacket with my name tag, then I hold babies for three hours. *I'm just a volunteer,* I say when a parent mistakenly asks me about medications, or when a doctor arrives to pass his flashlight across a baby's face. That "just" modifies me; I become a presence inconspicuous yet necessary as a ceiling tile, or a light.

I know nothing, and in lieu of knowledge I cultivate instinct. I slip through the halls, almost invisible, drawn by a baby's cry anywhere on the floor. I snap on the latex gloves. I bend and thread my arms through a tangle of i.v. lines and lift the child away from her crib. I back myself into a rocking chair, by now an expert at holding the array of tubing aloft, hardly noticing anymore the bandages, the bruises, the cuts. The baby might promptly fall asleep, but I go on rocking and rocking. I can't put her down, not yet. I know she feels me rocking even in her sleep. Her breath—sour and bitter—becomes my breath, her stuttering heart my own.

Or she might stay awake, gazing at me and wondering. I rock "Girl _____" for two hours. The motion reminds me of the davening of Jewish men at the front of the synagogue: the repeated half-bow to an unseen presence, the bodily gesture of prayer. The baby blinks slowly, her fingers tug at the oxygen tube in her nose, her pupils expand just slightly when they alight on my face. Three different i.v. bags dispense liquids drop by drop. The tubes converge into a single needle piercing the back of her hand, held rigid by a padded splint. A nurse beckons to me, so I lift the child back into her crib, place her on her side, and tuck a rolled blanket against her back. I watch her a few seconds more, my chest already cold with her absence. I know, if she's lucky, we'll never see each other again.

The nurse asks me to help pacify a distressed preemie, and I slip my hands through the gloves in the incubator and stroke a stomach the size of a newborn kitten's. He's crying, but I barely hear him through the plastic walls, and soon he settles down: his arms lie open at his side, his mouth shapes itself to an imaginary breast.

Around me, the ward projects an aura of stability—no emergencies here, no alarm. One floor above us lies Intensive Care: many of the babies descend from that plane, returned from the brink, their parents exhausted and pale. One floor below is the emergency room: many of the babies ascend from there, successfully returned from seizures, choking, concussion. Sandwiched between the floors of panic lies this base of equilibrium, with its multiple i.v. stands, chairs rocking, babies sleeping, every breath monitored, every pulse—many of the patients so small they're only a swell of blankets in the middle of these vast hospital cribs. We're surrounded by the mesh of protocol: nurses slip from task to task, swaddling a baby in an instant, stripping paper off thermometers, writing every observation in their charts—these actions merge into one, and they lull me into feeling that all is business as usual, nothing could really go wrong.

But in one of the isolation rooms a child is screaming: a little girl, two days old, born with no anus. "She poops out the same hole as she pees," the nurse cheerfully tells me, in case I need to change her. I sit in the rocking chair, holding the newborn as she grimaces. I can't help it, I become acutely conscious of my own body: my colon, my vagina, my rectum; I imagine how easy it would be for something to go wrong, for the parts not to match up completely. One small error, and a lifetime of pain, discomfort, complication. Maybe not even that. Maybe not a lifetime.

Sleeper couches fold out next to each crib, and often the floor space surrounding them is cluttered with overnight bags, magazines, bags of snacks. In these cribs, Polaroid photos of Mom and Dad hang at eye level, crayon drawings by siblings chirp *I love you!*, and colorful handmade blankets are tucked into corners.

When no parents stand at these bedsides, I wonder where they are. I wonder where I would be if my baby were in a hospital crib, attached to a monitor to make sure she was alive. If my baby were in the hospital for three months, would I have the stamina to sleep in one of these white leatherette chairs every night? Would I walk out-side under the blossoming cherry trees that line the driveway of Children's Hospital? Would I keep walking, down to Lake Washing-ton, and on and on, gulping the fresh air, trying not to scream? I don't know. I want to believe I would be at the bedside every minute, holding my child against my belly. But, yesterday I had a splitting headache, and I wanted nothing more than to put down the fussing baby at my shoulder. I wanted nothing more than to be unburdened beneath the cherry trees.

Most often the cribs I approach are steely blank, the baby wearing a hospital issue T-shirt, the only decoration on the crib an identi-fication card and a densely scribbled chart. No balloons, no photos, no drawings—only plain, flannel blankets from the hospital shelves. This naked bed usually signals that the child has been abandoned, left to the care of the hospital or the systems that stand in place for such infants. The parents cannot be found, or refuse to come, or are under arrest.

Today I walk by an isolation room where the I.D. card reads: "Doe, Jane." Beneath this card, a green slip of paper asks the parents or guardians of this child to come to admitting and fill out the requisite paperwork. I know this means the parents have disappeared. The shades are drawn; the door, closed. I hover a moment but hear no cry, nothing to demand my presence, so I move on, my hands pushed deep into the square pockets of my blue jacket.

In the next room there is a baby girl born too early, at thirty weeks, to a teenager who received no prenatal care. The baby's bones were so brittle most of them fractured during delivery; now she's almost blind, her lungs are malformed, her hearing damaged. But, two months out of the womb, she seems determined to live: she sucks on her bottle voraciously, tugging the nipple into her mouth, her eyes popping. The mother has not visited for three weeks, a student nurse tells me, and so I automatically hold the baby closer, whisper in her ear, as if she needs it more than the others, as if these few hours could somehow make up for a lifetime's worth of neglect.

When I get home I tell my boyfriend about this child, about her medical problems and the absent mother. He responds: "Why didn't she just get an abortion?" And since he has spoken my hidden thoughts, the ones I've tried to suppress all afternoon, I become angry and leave the dinner table. I go out on the front steps and cry. When he comes out to apologize, I say: *She is not an abstract concept anymore.*

After my three months on this floor, the question of abortion has become more troubling to me, has sharpened into the one essential question: when did the few, divided cells inside a teenaged girl become that baby whose weight I still felt in my arms? Certainly the girl might have been better off choosing abortion; perhaps her child is destined for nothing but a life of trouble and pain. But is there really some threshold between non-human and human that is crossed at three months, four months, or six? Does a fetus become human only when it looks like a person, with hands and fingers and hair? How do I explain the grief I still feel at my own miscarriages? The embryos were only four weeks old, but I still have the nagging sense that something—something human—has been irretrievably lost.

I have no answers, but I have too much time to question such things while I rock back and forth, these babies breathing rapidly in my arms. Some of them look as though they're still in the womb, they're that wrinkled and tenuous. I pat my hand rhythmically between their shoulder blades. I mimic an intrauterine heartbeat, giving the babies one overriding stimulus around which to organize chaos.

Sometimes they stop breathing a moment, suspended, and I panic. I nudge them a little, and their breath starts up, normal, smelling of milk. Their chapped lips twitch up into the reflex of a smile.

To volunteer, they say, is to be aligned with the fullness of your own volition. The term "volunteer" stems from the obsolete word "volunty" which means "that which one wishes or desires." You do this work because it comes from you naturally; if that impulse falters, you may stop, no questions asked. The volunteer tomatoes in my garden grow without any prompting from me; they arrive out of nowhere, and the volunteers are the hardiest ones, sticking it out long past the others have withered from drought or flood or disease.

We glance sideways at each other, us volunteers. We see the blue jackets out the corners of our eyes and nod. We come for different reasons, I know, though the motives all reduce to two or three identical lines on the application forms: *I want to give something back to the community. I love kids. I'm interested in being a doctor.* Hovering behind these lines are the other reasons: *I'm lonely. I'm childless. I want to feel as if I matter. I want to be missed when I'm gone.*

I don't know if I'm missed when I'm gone. I get in my car and remove the blue jacket, the name tag. My hands smell like baby, or of the soap at the ward sink, a vaguely nauseating combination of hospital and the insides of latex gloves lined with talc. My left arm will be sore for a day; I'll live the rest of the week mostly inside my office, writing, or going to the health club, riding my bicycle through the city streets to the bay. Then comes Tuesday. My schedule takes on a pleasing and necessary weight. "Tomorrow I'm at the hospital," I say to no one in particular, marking it again on the calendar.

Yesterday I held a baby who'd been beaten into a coma. I held her for my entire shift, her body unnaturally rigid, her cry like a cat's meow. Her nerves could still respond to pain, the nurse told me, but otherwise her brain was absent, her pupils fixed. She was six months old. "Doesn't look like she'll come out of it," the nurse said. She touched the baby's head gently, then left me alone with her. This girl seemed most comfortable nestled tightly against my side, while I remained motionless; any movement startled her reflexes and made her cry. Once, she sucked her pacifier for twenty minutes, this instinct bypassing the dead circuits in her brain. I memorized her eyelashes—deep black and impossibly long, curling against the ridge of her cheek.

I couldn't help but imagine the scene—the moment the large hand struck the soft spot at her temple, the impact, the crack of bone. I held her in the crook of my arm; I became rigid, like her, stiff as a catatonic. Hours later, when the nurses and I finally wedged the girl upright in bed, I saw her face full-on for the first time. She was awake: one eye wide open, the other halfway closed. Her pupils blank. Her tongue resting dumbly inside her mouth.

When I left the hospital, I sat in my car and cried from exhaustion and fury. I drove home, my hands white against the steering wheel. I made dinner. I went to a movie. My boyfriend said: "Perhaps you will be a blip on her memory, a second of comfort." Perhaps. "Do you know how," he said, "when you're sick, and what you remember from those days is the hour a cool breeze came through the curtains, cooling you? That moment of relief?"

More likely I'll be nothing, or only a part of the continuum of pain. All that night I felt this baby's weight on my arm. I remembered stroking her knee, her calf, her toes already stiff, as if in rigor mortis. I remembered that one eye, open wide, but focused on nothing. I could not reach her. While I stroked her, I tried to explain: *This is what touch can mean.*

I am there only once a week. I hold usually one baby, maybe two, sometimes three. How do these nurses bear it, the doctors? I want to ask them, but they're too busy. The babies keep coming, arriving from Intensive Care, from the emergency room. Like sponges, the babies absorb all a family's frustration, an entire community's pain. They emerge, tactile evidence of abstract phenomena: here is the mottled face of poverty, there the body of abuse. Here are the hands of racism, inequity, and impotence—bruised from the repeated probe of an i.v.

Today is my last day on the infant ward. I'm moving to Salt Lake City, and I know I'm going to miss these children more than I can say. The nurse, whose name I've never learned, has asked me to hold a little girl two months old, tiny as a newborn. This baby has a deep, phlegmy cough, so I need to wear a gown, gloves, and a full facial mask to feed her the bottle. She stares at me, astonished, grinning so much the nipple keeps popping from between her lips. The world to her is all eyes, looming above pink paper masks, and I can sense her trying to strip these masks away with the force of her gaze. She wears a hospital issue T-shirt, and socks that slither up her calves like leg warmers. No books, balloons, or drawings decorate her room. I see no name on her chart.

Who are you? I ask her, smiling under my mask. The nipple slides from her mouth. Her eyes are so bright I can hardly bear to look at them. They will burn me, I think, excavate all my fear and desire. But I lean a little closer to hear what she might say. Her arms wind-mill around her head—pointing out the window to the cherry trees, to the other babies, to the nurses, and back to me. She keeps her gaze steady on my face. *I am everything,* she laughs. *Who are you?*

Who am I? I am a woman holding a baby not my own. I take her weight, light as it is, and hold her the way mothers will always hold infants: close to the breast, the heart.

Raging Waters

Above me, the loudspeakers croon, *All that I need is the air that I breathe and to love you.* In this particular hour, at Raging Waters in Salt Lake City, everyone seems to believe it: the many children, and the adults who trot behind them, all of them wet and smiling, their bare legs and arms and belly buttons flashing through the heat. Some of them hoist pink rafts onto their shoulders; some drag blue tubes behind them; some have no rafts at all, just their damp feet slapping on the asphalt, their arms flung high as they slide down the chutes, through the fountains, tumbling into the frothy water. The crowd neither walks nor runs, but moves like one organism with many limbs; it undulates in all directions around the water slides, toward the snack bar, into the wave pool. A flock of boys scatters at the edge of the pool; teenage girls skitter by, the skin of their thighs and bellies radiant. Bathing suits punctuate this expanse of flesh like mere afterthought.

From where I've chosen to sit in the shade, in my black Land's End, Kindest-Cut tank, I have a clear view of the splashdowns from

Shotgun Falls, The Terminator, and several loop-de-loop affairs that wind down from on high, their sources impossible to decipher. One slide drops vertically into a pool; the riders tuck themselves onto yellow sleds and plummet down, then bounce across the surface of the water like a skipped rock. For an hour, I watch people zoom out of tunnels and plunge over waterfalls, their legs and arms akimbo, one person after another, skimming around curves, flying, arcing, descending, their screams merging into a pleasant, discordant harmony, like jazz.

Though hundreds of children roam the crowd, carrying with them the opportunity for any number of altercations, I hear no cries, no parents shouting, no slaps, no whines. In the line to the snack bar (hamburgers $2.50; pretzels $1.00), the children can have whatever they want; they clutch damp dollars in their fists and hop from foot to foot, towels draped over their shoulders, or tucked around their waists.

My charges have already melded into the crowd. Hannah and Sarah are not my children, though I've come to use the word "my" when I speak of them. I've known them for two years, but I have only a few weeks more to spend with them; I'll be moving to another state, leaving them behind with promises not to forget. Though I know we will, all of us. Already, I can hardly remember their faces, here in this crowd where all the children begin to look alike—their skin slick, their hair one damp color, their bathing suits askew on bodies that take no notice.

With Sarah, who is six, I've already been to Dinosaur Pond and swum among its sighing palms, slid through the primordial waters. We put our raft into the wave pool ("Utah's Beach") and rode the crest of the waves into shore. With the strength of someone twice her size, she tugged the raft back into deep water. Though she can't yet swim, she showed no fear as the waves broke over her head; she emerged from each one, her eyes wide, her mouth sputtering, her hands splayed at her sides. She staggered and fell back, like someone intoxicated; I lunged for her, but already she was up, laughing, her bathing suit straps down around her elbows. Her eyes, laser-bright, no longer looked out on this earthly world. I shouted her name, but she had eyes only for the water, searching the waves, baiting them to engulf her once again. Looking at her, I could imagine her face the day she was born: her mouth a puckered exclamation of both wonder and rage, her eyes gazing back to a place I'd never be able to fathom. I reached for her again, and she was slippery as a fish, or a newborn, sliding out of my grasp.

I think I could stay cheerfully on the lawn for the rest of the day, but Hannah, the nine-year-old, issues a challenge. *White Lightning.* She knows I'm afraid to go down the slides, we've discussed this. Before we came, I told her I'd had a bad experience on a crude water slide as a child; I've said there's no way I'm going down. But now she stands over me on the grass, her bikini dripping, her hands gripping her shoulders. She knows she has me; her face is alight. She reminds me that I've asked her and her sister to try something new every day. She reminds me I've told her to face her fears head on, to try whatever you think is impossible.

The first, and only, time I've been on a water slide was almost thirty years ago, when I was twelve years old. I remember the tall slide in an abandoned field outside L.A. No ponds, no dinosaurs, no carefully engineered drops: only a trickle of water splashing down a Plexiglas slope, with three plateaus spaced at irregular intervals. It reminded me of a vertical slip 'n' slide; the riders careened off onto a wet, plastic drop cloth spread over the grass.

I wore a bikini with a halter-top, the straps of which cut into the skin at the base of my neck. It was a hot, L.A. summer night, the air stagnant and thick, the vapor lights of a distant airfield shimmering through the smog. I climbed the ladder with my brother and his friends, those boys from the basketball team who made me breathless with a vague desire. I was aware of my body in the bikini as I climbed, the boys close behind me; I knew my legs were the finest part of me then, slender and long and tanned. I laughed carelessly as we reached the top, and turned to say something witty, but the boys pushed past me to grab their mats and hurtle down the slide, whooping. I watched them go, some of them head first, and in moments they became small distant bodies strewn across the grass. I paused a moment. My brother handed me a mat. "Go," he said, jerking his head. I crouched. He pushed me off, and I was sliding down, fast. Too fast.

No one had said anything about technique. No one had said this task required any finesse at all. I made the mistake of leaning forward at first, off balance, and as I gripped my mat, I *flew* down the side of that mountain, lifting off at each plateau and slamming down on my tailbone, bouncing up, skidding down. My body no longer belonged to me; it uncoiled into space, leaving me behind. At the bottom, when I finally veered off onto land, I was sobbing. Not whimpering in a sad, lady-like way, but crying big, snotty tears I wiped off with the flat of my hand. My brother and his friends already scrambled to go back up, but they hesitated, looking at me with their heads cocked to the side, as if I were a strange animal they'd never before encountered. They looked to my brother. I saw his lips twist with embarrassment as he held out his hand to help me up. "It's supposed to be *fun*," he hissed, and then let me go. The boys turned away en masse, their boxer shorts barely hugging their bony hips, their hairy calf muscles bulging as they climbed the ladder again.

It's supposed to be fun. All my life, it seems now, I've murmured that phrase to myself in the most unlikely places: on the playground as a child, at the mall as a teenager, even—as I've grown into middle age—during lovemaking with men both sweet and kind. I've said it with both wonder and despair, as if "fun" were a foreign term I've yet to fully comprehend.

Now, nearly thirty years later, I stand with Hannah on the steps to White Lightning. I don't think I've ever seen her so happy, and thus so beautiful; her entire body seems incandescent, lit up with her triumph at getting me here at all, on the wooden stairs high above Raging Waters. Her hair is plastered to her head, outlining the bones so perfectly joined; her belly, midway between a child's and an adolescent's, distends just slightly between the top and bottom halves of her bathing suit. She clutches the front end of our raft, leaning toward the next step up, and the next. We have a view of the entire Salt Lake Valley from here. A haze obscures the Wasatch Front and below us golfers tee off on the 18th hole.

Hannah and I watch slider after slider go down Blue Thunder, the slower of the two rides on this platform, the one most people choose. I look to the left, at White Lightning, at the tight curves and the three sharp descents, the waterfall roaring off the end. "Why isn't anyone going down this one?" I ask, trying to be casual, but my voice squeaks up a little, and Hannah grins. "It's *fast*," she says. "That's why."

Finally we're at the top. A Raging Waters "Guest Assistant," in her white polo shirt and royal-blue shorts, watches us with lazy boredom through her sunglasses. No expression mars her placid face as I situate the raft in the starting gate, no expression of warning or respect. I sit in the back of the raft, with Hannah between my legs, and I look up at the girl a moment, wanting *something* from her—a benediction, perhaps—but she gives us only a little push with her sneakered foot, and we're off.

We enter the first curve fast, sliding up on one wall then the other, straightening out for the first drop where we lift off, *oh god*, into the air, and we bump down hard, but no pain and no time to think of pain, the water rushing us through a tunnel and into the next drop, *please*, and the next; I'm holding on to Hannah and leaning back, *yes!*, as we're spit out into the waterfall. We're sailing over it. My body no longer seems linked to me; it's lifted free of gravity and become only motion and speed and liquid as Hannah and I splash down into the pool.

I'm laughing now, not crying, but laughing so hard I can barely speak. The waters roil and dump us off the raft. Hannah hops out of the pool. She stands taut on the edge, looking down at me, eagerness trembling in all her limbs. There is so much I want to say, so much I *could* say, but all I manage to sputter is: "*That* was so much *fun*."

Hannah nods, smug in her knowledge of what fun is, satisfied to be the one teaching *me* a lesson. She pulls the raft from the water, raises her lovely eyebrows. "Again?" she asks. I look up at her. The chlorine burns my eyes, but I can see Hannah more clearly than I ever have before. Unlike my vision of Sarah in the wave pool, which rocketed her back to an infant, I imagine Hannah far into the future, as a young woman, gazing with this same intensity at a horse, at a man, at her own child sleeping in her arms. The water magnifies everything about her—her brave lips, her high cheekbones, her capable hands—and makes me believe beyond all reason that I really will know her forever.

Other sliders release into the pool, all hallelujahs and hosannas, splashing me off my feet. So I hoist my heavy body onto the cement.

I sit there a moment, catching my breath, and the crowd throbs around me. It's grown larger but no less unified, feet slapping in every direction, voices raised in one keen avowal of fun. But Hannah is the only one to notice me here, a baptized convert in the midst of the masses. She's waiting for my answer. The tape on the loudspeaker has looped around full circle to *All that I need is the air that I breathe and to love you*. I can only nod my head yes, when what I mean is: Yes, my love, we'll do it again, and again, until the hours have spilled from this day and our time here is finally done.

Dirty Windows

The sun is out in Bellingham, Washington, which means that most women I know, including me, are staring at our dirty windows. Not *out* them, but *at* them. We're seeing the streaks, the smudges, the fingerprints, the coating of dust, the firm outlines of water drops left over from the hard rains of spring. We're looking up the phone number of our window cleaners—that nice couple with the VW bug—or we're considering the time and effort of getting out our own Windex, our rags, our squeegees, and spending this beautiful day spritzing, and wiping, and squeaking, and spritzing again.

Or we shift our gaze and see the inches of cat and dog hair in the corners of our wood floors, the fur spread like a second mat on the living room rug. We're seeing the cobwebs dangling from the corners of the ceilings, forming filaments of dirty lace across the tops of our cabinets. We're seeing the age spots on our hands, our unpedicured toes, the hair on our legs coarse and dark after a spring of long pants, leggings, and tights. We're seeing all the things that are normally covered up, or blissfully ignored, for most of our cloudy days in the northwest, that gray light so silver, so soft, so forgiving.

Perhaps that is why most of us feel drawn to live here, in the far north corner of the nation, with our preponderance of muted days; it's why we have migrated back here after brief sojourns in drier and sunnier lands—Southern California, Montana, Utah—places where the sun shines *a lot*, where the landscapes are certainly beautiful in their dry, vivid ways, but where we never feel truly at home. No, we say, give us cloud cover. A damp breeze. The smell of moist earth that greets you as you deplane on the tarmac of a tiny airport. Give us indirect light; we are plants that thrive in partial shade.

We sigh at our dirty windows, and we wonder if perhaps we've been aching inside, too, for a light that is a little more soft, more forgiving—a light that fusses about us and pulls our garments just so to hide any flaws. When I first started a meditation practice over thirty years ago, I expected that kind of shimmer, a gentle beam, but instead got the full brunt of direct light through dirty windows, a glare that makes you squint. You see every smudge on your character, every fingerprint on your soul, every trace of rains long gone. I closed my eyes, said my mantra, and wished for a cloudy day, one that might wash me in pearls. Such a thing never happened.

For many years now, my sitting meditation has diminished in favor of something else. I walk to yoga class three times a week, and in that walking I place my feet just so: *I have arrived*, I say on the in-breath, *I am home*, I say on the out-breath, and then the chest-nut trees, the blackberry bushes, seem to wave in acknowledgment, even if I do it just once, even if I'm present here in this world for just a few seconds at a time. Often I'm walking west at the time of day when the sun has just passed its zenith and is heading toward sunset. Sometimes I have to shade my eyes—on one of those rare days when there's nothing to filter the rays—but most often I can feel the lessening of the sun's intensity in those five minutes, the gathering of clouds on the horizon, the way some breeze far above makes them break apart in pleasing patterns that will, in an hour or so, deepen to a slow burn.

And in my yoga class my teacher tells us to bring the outside and the inside together as one. We become aware of small muscles, little ligaments, the breath filling us up and creating space where none ever existed. I bring my head to my knee, I salute the moon, and I make a mandala of my body on the little narrow mat. In Shivasana, the resting pose, I feel my teacher's hand on my head—a touch light and soft—and then it's gone. But I still feel it, the after-image of her palm, that touch of forgiveness wiping all the panes clean.

The Burden of Bearing Fruit

Last winter, we got some terrible windstorms. A huge willow down the street from me exploded in two: the top half flew into the street, and road crews closed off Cornwall for several hours as they cleaned up the mess. Then a thick old fir smashed through the roof of my friend's house, smack in the middle of her kitchen. The branches punched through the cupboards, reached in like craggy arms and broke her dishes. I stopped walking my dog in Cornwall Park—a thick grove of old growth cedars and firs—as every tree now looked like a weapon. The tops swayed in long arcs, and I wondered about the sturdiness of all those roots, at what point they might give way.

I eyed the trees around my house, squinting at them with suspicion. What about that hawthorn with its wizened, hollowed-out trunk? What about my own willow, the Rainier cherry? The Gravenstein apple stood far enough away from my house and the neighbor's so it wouldn't cause any harm should it topple, and the copper beech—well, it gave off an aura of invincibility, with its wide trunk, its no-nonsense leaves still clinging despite the storm.

The two main culprits: the hawthorn, a tree I had never liked because of its thorns, its messy berries in the fall, the not-quite-beautiful blossoms in the spring; and the cherry, a tree I adored. My neighbors planted it forty years earlier; Dorothy, now 98, once brought me the receipt to show me the sapling had cost $7.95 back then. Now it towered over the house with branches spindling out in every direction, a giant presence in my kitchen window I studied every morning and evening as I ate my solitary meals. In the spring, fat cherry blossoms swelled on the limbs, filled both my kitchen window and the upstairs view; in April, I could see the crown of my tree from blocks away as I drove home from work, and even after nine years this vision still gave me a flush of pride, an almost embarrassed satisfaction, as if the tree itself welcomed me home with trumpets and banners.

I couldn't imagine living without it, but many had already given this tree a death sentence: calcified streams of sap arced from every opening in the flakey bark, indicating disease, or parasites, or both. These sap icicles were beautiful in their own way—translucent, amber, and twisted into elegant shapes—but after a while they melted into sticky, viscous puddles on the grass. My arborist, Ruthie, told me in a note: "It's been an honor to work on this magnificent tree, but I'm sorry to tell you that she's terminal." The cherry had given up on providing fruit a few years ago, but still those blossoms arrived every spring—heraldic, triumphant.

Decades ago, I saw a tree fall in the forest. I lived then at Orr Hot Springs, in northern California, a place situated in a steep river valley that leads to the sea. During winter storms, the river rose to dangerous levels, coursing in muddy waves below the bridge, and everything stayed damp: woodpiles, shoes, overcoats, hair. Down the road, an old-growth redwood grove stood protected, and we often walked those paths in the rain to feel the contradictory dryness in the undergrowth.

One day, I walked along the road toward the grove with my lover. I hate the word "lover" but it's the only descriptor for this particular paramour; he was married, to my best friend, but before you judge me too harshly, let me confess that we were all in this together—that my best friend held a dalliance with my live-in boyfriend too, and we had all gamely agreed to this arrangement, giddily, like children making up rules in a tree house. And this was the eighties, in northern California, a place where oddballs had always gravitated; our little "experiment" didn't seem so strange. We all lived together in a community that revolved around the hot springs and our small business; a sign on the front gate declared: "Warning, you may encounter nudity beyond this point." We took turns cleaning the centuries-old bathhouse, the swimming pool, the sauna. We took turns at the front desk, an enormous slab of redwood polished to a high shine.

Still, especially in the winter, we had a lot of time on our hands. We made clear ground rules, met a few times in each others' houses after eating good meals and drinking wine from the local vineyards. We did Tarot readings to divine the suitability of this arrangement, threw the I Ching, and while the answers were ambiguous, as they always are with these kinds of things, we chose to interpret them as "thumbs up!"

Only this man and I, we knew we were making up our own rules as we went along; we weren't supposed to fall *in* love. We weren't supposed to have secret trysts without them.

But here we were, walking along a deserted road in the rain, holding hands. The ditches at the edge of the road filled like moats, and we could hear the evergreens shifting in the wind. The gray air smelled of resin and wildflowers, though the wildflower bloom was still a good month off. Then the rain let up a bit, and we took off our hoods to hear each other better, as we were having a lovers' quarrel. Something about whether we should continue doing what we were doing, whether any good could ever come of it, what about commitments, what about children, what about our futures, what about, what about?

A crack in the woods. Gunshot? We stopped a minute to listen. Hunters sometimes came up our road after deer, though deer season was a long way off. They hunted turkeys. They hunted wild boar. Sometimes they just wanted to hold target practice against the trunks of the old trees. The crack widened, turned into a long quavery moan, and we heard the tree falling before we saw it. A big tree. A tree that disrupted the canopy in a messy shower of leaves and branches, falling with a swish and a thwump on the road in front of us. A huge fir tree, a good five feet across, spanning the entire road—roots upended on the right, crown lost in the creek to the left, high branches waving in a spray of wet needles.

One moment, a clear road ahead; the next, an enormous obstacle, a body flung to block our way. I felt the road sway and shake, and my knees buckled. I felt the vibration of the tree's fall all the way up to my throat. If we had kept walking, kept holding hands, kept going down this path, the tree would have smashed us flat.

Even now, years later, I can feel it: the smell of sap burns in my nose, hot and sharp in the midst of the cold, as if by falling the tree set itself on fire. And out of my mouth blurts, *I'm sorry!* My lover, his mouth still gaping at the enormous tree, turns to me, says, What? What are you sorry for? *For everything*, I say, and I turn and start to hurry back up the road, back toward home. I want to tell my friend

I'm sorry. I want to tell her everything, and I want to keep my hands off her husband, and I want my boyfriend back, and can I brush her hair? My friend trots to keep up with me, keeps asking *what? why?*, and I can't explain it to him, not yet. But I will. Soon, I'll tell him that the tree seemed clearly an oracle, telling us to stop—stop what we're doing and go back.

When I bought my house, the cherry tree was laden with small green fruits, a luring promise. I bought the house in a flood of adrenaline—a single woman making a huge decision without anyone else as a buffer. It felt a little too much like giving in: finally buying my own house because I still hadn't married, still hadn't made a family. Some people told me this purchase would be a death knell for future relationships, that no prospective boyfriend would want to get involved since I'd already obviously declared I plan to be single *forever*. I wanted to retort, but didn't, that maybe buying a home just meant I want a roof over my head, *forever*.

When I first stepped into that little cottage on Cornwall Avenue, I got the "feeling" I'd heard so much about from other homeowners, a bodily sign that a house is yours. It descended upon me like a visitation—neither a tingle nor a flutter, but more like an infusion, a wave of contentment and desire most similar to a blush in the presence of someone you like. Someone you like *a lot*. I looked inside the two small bedrooms, I peered into the minuscule bathroom, I wandered upstairs to the attic loft just large enough to stand up in. I peered out that window into the branches of the Rainier cherry. The house, I could tell, really was only big enough for one, but one seemed like enough for now.

All this time my realtor Julie, sensing the nearness of the Holy Spirit, had wisely kept her distance, allowing the house and me a little one-on-one time on our own. But now she sat across the room from me and murmured, "It's a good buy, such a great location, and what a yard!" It's true, the yard was long, large, green, bordered by a field of blackberries in the back, punctuated by both that cherry tree, and a Gravenstein apple near the back fence. Just a few feet away, the city rose garden startled in full bloom, in view of my front porch, as if the city employed a crew of expert gardeners to plant and prune and mulch, expressly for my own enjoyment.

I signed the papers, I cried for days, then set about making it my home. Everyone who came over said of the cherry, "great tree," especially in July, when it started ripening its fruit. I watched the squirrels and the birds take the lion's share, mocking me by dropping half-eaten cherries to the patio and the lawn. I ate only the low-hanging cherries, the ones I could reach simply by pulling down a branch and plucking. I'd had Rainier cherries from the store, but these fruits were a surprise: the flesh so sweet and yet so complex, the firm skin giving way to the textured meat beneath. Almost like a golden plum, but small and round and mine. The tree put out too much fruit for one person, so I invited over friends to come with buckets, bags, colanders and take whatever they liked.

My friend Bruce clambered into the tree and shook the branches jubilantly, showering cherries and bruising nearly every one of them, but we gathered them anyway and ate and ate. My friend Nancy came over with Tupperware. I brought baggies full of them as offerings to my co-workers. My puppy, in her first summer with me, eager to try anything that would fit in her mouth, delicately took cherry after cherry on her tongue, and later I'd find piles of poop studded with oval pits. Certain this couldn't be good for her, I maniacally swept them up several times a day, only to have more and more of them rain down.

Every April my cherry bloomed, and every April my parents called to ask, *how's the cherry doing?* And I would say, *it's brilliant.* I told them it made me so happy. *If you're happy, we're happy,* is what they've always say to me, though there's the unspoken addendum, the question, *but are you* really *happy?* What I don't say: The tree makes me feel less alone. It makes me feel as though I've done something right.

When I was growing up, we had an olive tree in our front yard, right outside the kitchen window. The waxy leaves always stayed green, and the olives didn't seem like fruit so much as nubs of errant flesh that stained our feet, our shoes, left big red splotches on the walkways leading to the front door. They caused our mother to be vigilant, and I picture her on the front walkway, perpetually sweeping, and at the front door, sweeping off our feet before we could come inside. Inevitably, though, some splotches made their way onto the kitchen linoleum, the shag carpet—stains that never completely wore off.

It's funny now to think of it, having a tree bearing fruit that no one could eat. We were warned, constantly: don't eat them, they're poison! It was fruit that needed care. It was fruit that needed to be *cured,* a word I thought meant the olives needed to be healed of some disease, and in a way I was right. Curing involves softening, allowing the olives to release all their bitterness into salt. But I thrilled at the thought of it: *poison!* Sometimes I would touch a hard olive to my mouth, rub it against my lips. I'm sure my brother must have thrown some at me, and the UPS man probably cursed them on his trips to our front door.

There's a photo of me at three years old, wearing a nice outfit with a little jacket and Mary Jane shoes, my hair freshly cut in a bob to my chin. I'm standing on that walkway in front of the messy olive tree, looking toward someone—my mother? I'm smiling so hard my face looks like it will explode. The walkway has been swept clean, or perhaps the tree is still too young to bristle with poisonous fruit. I am young; I do not yet bristle at all. My parents wait for me to stop smiling so we can go wherever it is we need to go.

Why didn't they cut down that tree?, I wonder now. What kept them maintaining a tree that only caused aggravation? It must have been those evergreen leaves. Or the whiff of the Mediterranean, the mythic fruit, sacred olive, symbol of peace. What is sacred is often messy, I understand that now. What bears fruit always requires some patience, a love that's loyal and unremitting.

I imagine my mother at her kitchen table, looking at that olive tree day after day for thirty-five years. She is alone: husband at work, children at school, dog in her grave. The ironing board is set up behind her, a basket of rumpled shirts beneath it. She's drinking her second cup of coffee, toying with her teaspoon. The clock ticks. Any minute now, she'll turn on the radio, turn to her tasks. But for now she watches her street through the branches of that olive tree— the sleek green leaves, the treacherous fruit—and enjoys the way it shades her, keeps her just a little bit hidden.

In 2007, when I return home from a vacation in early July, my cherry tree is putting out a record crop: never before have I been able to grab so many with so little effort, which paradoxically makes me want to expend even *more* effort, get out the ladder from my neighbor's shed and climb up into the higher branches where the yellow-red fruit dangles in fat clusters.

It's the last crop my tree will put out, but I don't yet know this. I don't realize this display has all the makings of a last hurrah. I just know that for the first time I really want to gather them all, because these cherries make me recall the blossoms too, and lying on the sloping lawn under the tree in April with a man I thought I loved and his three sons. The boys were happy; they lay under the branches and noted the way the pink glowed against the blue sky, then clambered up and into the limbs to feel the blossoms against their skin. I promised we would all pick the crop in summer, a dangerous statement I understand now—implying some commitment, some future that naturally included a man and his three sons.

And now the season has turned, and the cherries are trembling in the rain, slowly going to waste if I don't pick them all myself soon. If the boys were here—in the scenario I pictured so often—I know we would gorge ourselves on cherries. The eight-year-old would scramble up into the tree's interior, and the thirteen-year-old would jump at the branches, and the sixteen-year-old would feign nonchalance as he bends a branch and so casually plucks.

And their father? I imagine him hanging back, his arms crossed, leaning against the carport, just watching. Or maybe he would be the one in the ladder, risking danger, handing down handfuls and handfuls of the fruit to his children who look up to him in the branches, shrieking "dad, dad, dad!" and hopping around with their buckets and bowls, wanting to catch the full measure of this bounty he's suddenly so willing to give.

Or maybe *I* would be the one just watching, already tired of cherries and the mess they make on the patio.

Now, alone in the summer, I pick the cherries by the pound and bring them in zip-lock bags to whoever will take them. And when the cherries keep offering themselves, ceaselessly, I will buy a cherry pitter and spend hours in my kitchen, breathing heavily as I pit them one by one, lay them out on a cookie sheet to be frozen and preserved. But what I really want to preserve, I know, are those un-tainted days—the weeks of blossom, the scent of incipient cherry—before you have to deal with all the fruit, the effulgence of it, the way it tastes so good the first bite and the next and the next, but eventu-ally becomes something you just have to give away.

My friend from Orr Springs is still my friend. She divorced her hus-band many years ago (not because of me), and remarried; she now lives on forty acres high in the dry-grass hills above Orr Springs. She and her current husband have created a homestead off the grid, an octagonal house that uses solar power, spring water, propane.

For a long time, their only shower was on the roof outside, under the umbrella of a large pacific madrone. Whenever I visit, I can't wait to take a shower there, to undress and step outside, feel the warm water and cool air mixing on my skin. It's here I feel most vibrant, completely myself in the company of orange bark, glossy leaves. The trees surrounding this shower seemed friendly enough; they sway in whatever breeze is handy.

The last time I visited my friend, I came for her son's wedding, a boy who has been my unofficial godson for twenty-four years, since the day he was born. The night before the wedding, we walked the ranch road to see the damage from the wildfires that had almost destroyed everything a month earlier, and she especially wanted to show me the blackened hills from the controlled burns started by the hundreds of firefighters who arrived to save the community. The controlled burns are meant to stop the wildfire in its tracks, "fighting fire with fire": a term I never understood until that moment, seeing the incomprehensible wide swaths of burnt hillside sweeping up from the valley. We both started to cry when she told me the fire "jumped the road," the worst thing that could happen, how they all could have been trapped behind a canopy of blazing manzanita. They spent days and nights clearing trees and brush from near the house to create a fire break, breathing in smoke; at one point they had to evacuate quickly, not knowing if they'd be able to return.

As we walked, the moon rose with Venus trailing at its side, illuminating this landscape I've loved for a long time. In this light, we stood there gazing at the damage, danger still a lurking presence in the air. There were wild turkeys in the brush behind the house, startling the quiet, scrambling into the meadow looking for food.

The next day we would travel south an hour to witness her son's wedding; the ex-husband will be there, looking handsome, and so will my ex-boyfriend, and whenever the four of us are together in the same place we get a little sheepish and giddy, still a little fevered from our long-extinguished flame. All four of us will sit together at a table, and while we won't really reminisce about the old days—nearly thirty years gone—we will feel that sense of being part of one another in ways that ordinary friendships can't really master.

The groom will be tall and self-assured, dancing with his new wife like a man who knows how to handle a woman, something that will surprise me, since I still see him as a rambunctious three-year-old boy who crawled into my lap, put his face right up to mine, and kissed me flat on the lips with an exaggerated smack. He used to tell complicated, absurd jokes that weren't funny, then pause, expectantly, for laughter. We liked to rub noses, didn't even care about snot.

At the wedding, someone will snap a picture of the four of us adults, ex-lovers, and when I study it later, we look so much ourselves, but with a worn patina overlaid on our faces, the eyes a little more tired. It will be late; we'll all be a little drunk from wine and dancing. So, we'll look happy. We'll look as if nothing has ever harmed us. Back at Orr Springs, we had once taken a "family portrait" in the nude, the four of us sitting on the floor of my friend's house in various poses of allure, the flash capturing my shy smile, my tiny breasts. We had leaned in toward one another, our heads touching, not unlike this wedding photo so many years later, all of us fully clothed, all of us laughing.

I never told my friend about that falling tree, about the way the force of it startled me out of my complacency and made me run to her for absolution. I never told her how alone I felt in that walk back up the road, even with her husband beside me, how I knew even then it would mean the end of everything: me and my boyfriend, her and husband, me and her husband, her and my boyfriend—it was all just so *complicated*, and I needed to get my life back to normal, there in a valley sheltered by trees. Eventually I knew I'd be leaving that valley, driving out in a battered truck loaded with books and pillows, looking for a different kind of family. I never told her any of this; I told her only that I was back, that we had come home.

In December, between windstorms, I decide both the hawthorn and the cherry need to be cut down, proactively, before they fall and damage my house or my neighbor's. I sleep uneasily, aware of the wind, of any creak of branch or twig. Many homeowners feel the same way, and by now landscapers cruise the neighborhoods, leaving cards with promises of quality tree removal.

I end up using a guy named Innocencio, from Hosanna Tree Service, and yes he wears a big cross, and yes, his business card declares he does all his work as service to the Lord. I figure it couldn't hurt to have a man of God up in the branches of my trees and, besides, he quoted me a good price.

In the week before he arrives with his crew, I try to say goodbye to the cherry tree, but I don't quite know how. It feels like a betrayal, to kill this damaged tree that has persevered for so long outside my kitchen window, kept me company in the spring, poured out beauty even when I was too low to notice. "These fruiting cherries," Innocencio said, "they don't really last too long in our climate. Better to have the ornamentals, they're hardier, they've got stamina." I circle the tree, I touch its sticky tendrils of sap. I pick a small branch up off the ground, thinking I'll enshrine it in a vase, but the branch apart from the tree is actually rather ugly and messy, and so I drop it and brush off my hands.

I'm hoping I'll be gone when the actual felling happens, but I'm home as Innocencio backs up his large truck, the one with a crane and a bucket, and I can't help but watch as they begin. I'm at the picture window in the kitchen, standing back just a bit because for some reason I don't want the crew to know I'm watching. In my mind I'd pictured the tree falling as one unit, a dramatic crash like that one on Orr Springs Road so many years ago, but of course this is a controlled cutting, performed in increments, bit by bit.

With expert speed Innocencio cranks the bucket into the highest limbs, revs the chainsaw and begins to cut with smooth, precise slices; the branches fall to his helpmates below, two young men in hard hats who scurry to pick up the large branches, piling them into manageable heaps. They keep their gaze up, even while they grab the wood. Before too long—too quickly—the tree is reduced to an amputated trunk rising about six feet tall. Innocencio gets down off the bucket and brings out the big gun: a huge chainsaw that he muscles into the trunk, reducing it to six equal logs in about five minutes, planing the remaining stump level to the ground.

It's breathtaking. And a little sickening. I go outside, out front, for some air, and the guys are taking a break too, going to their truck for water. I tell one of them I feel badly about cutting down that tree, and he grins at me. "Don't worry," he says, "if it makes you feel better, this job means I can buy Christmas gifts for my kids." I know it should, but for some reason it does not make me feel better, imagining his children playing with video games bought with blood money from my tree.

Before they leave I squirrel away a little chunk of the wood from a round branch, flakey moss clinging to the dry bark. It's surprisingly heavy for a small piece of wood, and I place it on my back steps until I can decide what to do with it next.

I write Innocencio a check, hand it over to him. He's a stocky guy, with a mustache and lots of chest hair; the muscles in his arms show that he's felled a lot of trees in his time. He seems to understand my silence. He says, gently, "It was good that tree came down." And I nod, thank him, tell him goodbye. When I go back inside, the picture window is blank. The stump of the tree glares. Sawdust powders the lawn. For days, weeks, afterward, whenever I drive into the carport, I'll startle a little at that empty expanse where my tree should be. I'll see that little piece of cherry wood, my souvenir, feel an urge to touch it the way I'm supposed to touch the *mezuzah* on the front lintel of my house—an acknowledgment of blessing, subservience, gratitude.

I miss my tree, I write to friends on Facebook. They send me sympathy notes, virtual pats on the back, frowny faces. Everyone seems to understand something I could never quite comprehend: how a lone tree can be a companion, how its sentience can harbor your own.

A week or so later I go upstairs, for what I can't remember: a book, perhaps, or to look at my meditation cushion and feel guilty for not meditating. The upstairs has been taken over by my cat, Madrona;

she sits imperiously on the recliner, twitching her tail when I appear, and drifts of cat hair pile up on the steps. It's four o'clock, just at sunset on this winter day, and when I go upstairs it all seems unfamiliar to me. Then I get it: the light.

With the cherry gone in back, the hawthorn gone in front, a new light comes in through the front and back windows, clean and undappled. I stop a minute on the landing and look west, across the space that used to hold the craggy cherry branches. I can see almost all the way to Bellingham Bay, and Lummi Mountain rises on the horizon. I don't feel so guilty anymore.

Instead, I start to plan a new dining room addition to my house. I've been here nine years, and there's nowhere for anyone to sit. Though I live alone—and probably will *forever*—I do love a good dinner party. My friends and I eat Hanukkah brisket on the floor around the coffee table; we stand up and slurp bowls of soup. The downed cherry tree has opened the whole back side of the house. I imagine a dining room, light and airy, with French doors leading out onto a deck. We'll cover over that stump, or perhaps pull it out; in any case, it won't even exist. I'm already thinking of the flowering dogwood that might take its place. Or an ornamental cherry, so much more hardy, without the burden of bearing fruit.

AT THE EDGE OF THE WORLD

Hungers

For me, reading and hunger have always been linked. I checked out ten books at a time from the local library and read in my small bedroom, oblivious to the sunny backyard outside my window. I rapidly turned the pages, my eyes barely scanning the words as I absorbed their meaning. *A Wrinkle in Time*, *The Wizard of Oz*, *The Borrowers*, an entire set of *Nancy Drew* mysteries: all these books disappeared inside me and left a small ache—like meals gobbled too fast. I always found myself slowing down toward the end, my thumb and forefinger resting for a long while on the tips of the closing pages before gradually, reluctantly, turning. Out the corner of my eye I saw the white space at the bottom of the last page, an abyss that signaled the end.

The passages about food exerted a mysterious power and stayed with me long after I'd finished. Even the description of the slop fed to the pigs in *Charlotte's Web* fascinated me—that strange mix of porridge with rinds of crusty bread, blackened orange peels, rotting apples. I could still feel Wilbur's visceral pleasure as he pushed his snout into the damp mess, and I admired Templeton's expertise at stealing and hoarding the choicest bits for his own. I remember reading *Winnie the Pooh* only for the pleasure of imagining my own paw scooping big gobs of honey onto my tongue. I begged my mother to buy a golden jar of honey, though we really had no need for it; we were a grape jelly kind of family, a white-sugar-in-the-Folgers kind of tribe. She relented one day and brought home a small honey bear, but of course when I squeezed out a thin stream onto my slice of Wonder bread, it bore scant relation to the meal I imagined Winnie and his friends enjoyed: the honey scooped warm from the heart of a tree, redolent of clover and wildflowers.

I had a penchant for stories of vagabond children and animals; there were many such books in those days, quest narratives of children banished from families or kingdoms, trudging silently away with only a small bundle tied to their backs. Or tales of heroic animals who had lost the humans who cared for them, picking their way through harsh landscapes and fierce weather. As I read, I wailed to myself: "But what will they *eat?*" and I anxiously gripped the already grubby pages of my book as I took in the accounts of wild potatoes gouged from the hardpan earth, the delicate flowers plucked from a stem and set on a tongue to dissolve. I came away from these books with a hunger no food could satisfy, and I wandered into my mother's kitchen, stricken and starved, to stare at the twelve boxes of cereal that lined the cabinet above the stove.

My reading led me to crave strange foods from which, in real life, I would surely have recoiled: hot milk and bread in a Swiss Alps chalet, tapioca pudding, shepherd's pie. As I grew older, and my tastes in reading became slightly more sophisticated, I read Perry Mason novels and once became obsessed with the description of a hurried lunch his assistant, Della Street, eats during the heady and frantic preparations for a murder trial: a steak sandwich, the meat sliced on a white roll spread thickly with butter and ketchup. Butter and ketchup? Such a combination seemed odd, vaguely erotic, and even now I imagine the butter and bread and meat and ketchup, each layer distinct yet melding into one, delectable whole. I couldn't find that passage now if you paid me (perhaps it was in *The Case of the Crying Swallow* or *The Case of the Careless Cupid*), but I'd bet money Erle Stanley Gardner lingered just a touch on that scene, enjoying this brief repast in writing. I'd bet that he put down his pen and went into his kitchen, peered into the refrigerator, hoping for some leftover meat, a bit of butter, a chunk of bread to satisfy the hunger his own pen had aroused.

Sometimes, when I knew a book would make me cry (*Charlotte's Web*, say), I ventured out of my bedroom, book in hand, and made my way to the footstool in my mother's kitchen. I said nothing, but perched there, hunched over my book, while my mother bustled about the counter and stove. With my eyes on the page, I heard the whoosh of the refrigerator door opened and closed, the precise clicks of the magnets catching on the cabinets, a discordant jostle of pots and pans. Something began crackling in a fry pan; my mother ran water in the sink. I read about Charlotte's noble death, her baby spiders floating away on silk balloons, an earthly reincarnation of all that is generous and fine. I began to sniffle, loudly enough so my mother would notice, and by the time I came to the last lines—"*It is not often that someone comes along who is a true friend and a good writer. Charlotte was both.*"—I was in full sobs, my mother's arms around me, her apron smelling of dinner.

It's not surprising, then, that I would eventually become both a cook and a writer, driven by the twin pleasures of palate and imagination. The first thing I consciously remember cooking was Pillsbury cinnamon rolls: those odd confections that please more for the *idea* of them rather than the reality, a creation born of packaging and the tactile pleasure such wrapping bestows. I remember gripping the hefty, cool tube, while my mother greased the round cake pan with Crisco. Already I felt a tingly anticipation: the nascent rolls nestled so neatly and tightly inside their compartment, ready to be released with one well-timed *thwack* on the edge of the kitchen counter. The rolls swelled out from the mangled cardboard, sticky and soft. My mother and I placed them carefully in the pan, their shoulders nudging, and slid them into the oven. We set the squat timer for 20 minutes, and I dragged over the kitchen stool to watch the rolls cook through the oven window. I watched that sooty pane of glass with rapt attention, the minutes ticking away to the *Ding!* of revelation. Aroma began to penetrate the kitchen—not exactly cinnamon as I would come to know it in my more discerning years as a cook, but an artificial spice mingled with dough and sugar. Even before the timer let out its happy sound, I was busy imagining the perfect, brown spiral and the icing that waited in its concise and clear little tub.

I remember my mother and I silently and secretly eating these rolls together, the boys of the house somehow banished. This surely can't be true: the smell of the baking rolls must have drawn my two brothers and my father into the kitchen, all of them in their boyish pajamas, rubbing the sleep from their eyes. They must have clamored for the rolls, grabbed them from the pan with their bare fingers. They must have swallowed them practically whole, foregoing the practiced refined gestures of unwinding those perfect spirals to reveal their sweet cores. Perhaps because of this very sacrilege, I stubbornly hold onto this fiction of my mother and me in a blessed communion, eating these rolls together in a warm kitchen, alone.

Or perhaps I associate all things cinnamon with my mother because she used to take me to the coffee shop at Bullock's Department Store, just the two of us, after we'd both had our hair cut at the store's in-house beauty salon. We sat at the counter, where the waitresses, dressed in blue with lacy aprons across their laps, immediately filled my mother's coffee cup and took my order for cinnamon toast. Never since have I found or been able to replicate this particular toast: it arrived, two white bread slices perfectly browned, each cut neatly in two triangles. The cinnamon and butter and sugar did not exactly melt *into* the bread as swim on *top* of it, creating an ambrosial liquid that coated my lips and my tongue. My newly cut hair swung against my jaw as I ate, and my mother held that coffee cup to her lips with both hands, watching the waitresses as they bustled about behind the counter. There was something unfathomable in her eyes those days, some private melancholy to which I was not privy. The taste of cinnamon lingered in my mouth the rest of the afternoon, while my mother held my hand and led me past shop windows with their bright displays that promised the world.

Ironically enough, I almost failed Home Ec in junior high school, bumbling my way through a series of cooking disasters that resulted in leaden baking powder biscuits and an odd dish that involved canned chili stuffed into Pillsbury popover rolls. We sweated in a prefabricated kitchen with deep tin sinks and slick Formica counters, pasteboard cupboards and plastic coffee cups with matching saucers. I almost always left this dreadful classroom in tears.

In the summer after my first year of junior high, my mother took me to a "box lunch auction" at a neighbor's house. At these auctions, young men in various stages of desirability "bid" on lunches that we girls had prepared and packaged in enticing, mysterious boxes. The boy then had the dubious honor of eating said lunch with the girl who made it: an equation made between the alluring qualities of the box's wrappings in direct proportion to the scrumptious lunch within. The boy could only hope that the bearer of this box lunch proved equally alluring on the outside, just as substantial on the inside. What an odd rite, as I remember it now: the boxes winked and glittered on the high table at the front of the lawn while someone's mother picked them up one at a time and held them high above her head. The boys called out their bids, each one inching higher until the winner was declared.

I don't remember what we fixed, my mother and I, but I remember the heated flush in my cheeks as my box came into view, wrapped in a broad red ribbon, much plainer than the sequin-bedecked box that had preceded me. The bidding, prompted by the auctioneer, was sporadic, but I remember quite clearly the poor boy who "won" me. He was cute enough, with short blond hair and a collared shirt buttoned up to the neck, but his miserable eyes gazed past me as we sat together on the grass, munching down our sandwiches, chewing and chewing, emitting loud gulping sounds as we swallowed. This food, for me, provided neither taste nor sustenance, put as it was to such utilitarian, and faintly tawdry, service.

Luckily I managed to mature into a fairly decent cook, and my favorite reading became cookbooks of all sorts: vegetarian, Indian, Mexican, all-American. I absorbed them with the same furious attention I gave to my storybooks as a child. Cookbooks now offered the same thrill as narrative: the set-up of the story, the avenues into any number of possible outcomes. I cooked the way that I lived: whole-heartedly, kindly, full of good intent. I had many friends who cooked this way as well, and I always loved going into houses that smelled of spices in glass jars, of wood smoke, of curry from a meal eaten days earlier.

One always knew a kindred house by the cookbooks on the kitchen shelf: the battered *Moosewood* missing its back cover, opening automatically to the Black Bean Soup or the Eggplant Mousakka; or the *New York Times Natural Foods Cookbook*, with its earnest recipes for Macrobiotic Super Soup with Buckwheat Dumplings, or Bone Marrow Gruel. *Vegetarian Epicure, The Silver Palate, Tofu Cookery, The Joy of Cooking*: these books were *used*, fondled, and loved. Those people whose cookbooks were hardcover and immaculate could not to be trusted; one entered their kitchens warily, sniffing for signs of life, and perched uneasily on their upholstered stools, fingering a glass of wine.

So many of my favorite moments have been spent in a kitchen among a friendly disarray, the cookbooks splayed open on a counter messy with tomato juice and bits of parsley. I chopped garlic and mushrooms on someone else's cutting board, talking in rhythm to the staccato of my knife, while somewhere behind me I could hear my friend moving in easy grace from sink to stove to fridge and back again. And then I sat, apron still on, at the kitchen table, while my friend leaned her elbows on the counter and studied the cookbook, not so much for exact instruction but for a general idea. We seasoned our stews and casseroles by instinct and smell alone, leaned over the steaming pots and took deep breaths, then added a palmful of basil, a pinch of marjoram, a splash of wine. And then the wait: the kitchen warm, the windows steamed, our hair curling of its own volition. During that interval, we told each other our troubles, and we did so in the form of story: weaving tales with full-fledged characters, advancing plots, well-placed flashbacks, the inevitable but surprising conclusions. When our troubles grew overwhelming, we coddled each other with comfort food: pureed soups, bread pudding, creamy pastas—food that required little effort to eat and returned us to the realm of our childhood, when all we had to do was open our mouths to be filled.

We went out to see movies like *Babette's Feast* and came home laden with blocks of Asiago cheese, crisp apples, the softest French bread, and ate and ate with our fingers for hours at a time. The more we ate the more hungry we became, as if this food merely dissolved into the flesh, leaving no remnant of itself behind. And woe to the unlucky one who had no lover, for after such a repast only a slow, languid session of lovemaking would do as a fitting and elegant dessert.

Love and food: those first timid gestures toward intimacy almost always come with forks hovering over laden plates, the glances over a glass of wine held too long at the lips. And when that intimacy erodes, it's not the bedroom that feels most desolate to me: it's the kitchen. Imagination flees, and I'm left with scrambled eggs, wan salads, microwaved baked potatoes. I keep using the same bowl, the same plate from the dish drainer. I carry my meals to the single place-mat on the kitchen table and spoon the food into my mouth, perus-ing whatever kind of reading matter I can find: the insurance circular, a day old newspaper, the personal ads. I take a few bites and chew, wipe the salad dressing from my lips, turn a page of the magazine, take another bite, and before I know it another meal has passed. I carry the plate and glass back to the kitchen sink, run water over them, and turn back to the empty house. My cookbooks, dusty and silent on the shelf, issue a reproach almost too grievous to bear.

My first real job entailed cooking for fifty children and their counsel-ors at a summer camp in northern California. Two acres of vegetable gardens provided most of our ingredients, and I remember running to the cornfield in my Birkenstocks, an empty woven basket at my hip, the kettle already on at full boil, and tearing fifty fat cobs off their stalks. I conscripted a few eager huskers, and in no time we threw the naked corn in the boiling water for a scant 3 minutes before bearing it with pride to the picnic tables. Throughout that summer, the children could have whatever they wanted, as long as we made it from scratch, so I learned how to make marshmallows, English muffins, bagels, our own cottage cheese. At night I went to bed with my cookbooks, reading them with the same avid attention I might give to a novel, blinking my heavy eyelids so I could make it through one more page. During the day, I made enormous pans of lasagna, vats of tomato soup, platters of stuffed zucchini, bubbling casseroles of macaroni and cheese. I leaned over the pots with my eyes closed, discerning the scents of dill, oregano, basil, even salt. I'm sure I looked odd, the way I passed my flared nostrils above the open pots, inhaling deeply as if in a trance.

Years later, I cooked for a 10-day meditation retreat conducted in silence. I had attended such retreats myself and so knew the routine: breakfast at 6 a.m., usually a hot porridge with fruit and soy milk on the side, followed by the main meal at 11:00 A.M., something light and simple, and then no food at all for the rest of the day, save for a cup of tea and a piece of fruit at 4:00. As a participant in these retreats, I had usually focused all my anxieties on food and the lack thereof: dreaming in meditation about fat burritos stuffed with chicken, or pizzas dripping with cheese. I fantasized about food so vividly—steaming platters of enchiladas, heaped bowls of chow mein, glistening chocolate frosted éclairs—that I gasped with both surprise and disappointment when the bell rang, signaling the end of this reverie and a return to the austerity of the dining room, with its chaste white platters of tofu stir fry.

So, when I was offered the chance to cook at a retreat held in a Marin County farmhouse, I brought all my creative energy to bear on that late morning meal, wanting, in a way that was wholly non-Buddhist, for my food to reap silent praise and hosannas. I knew what went on behind those serene visages; I knew that the stomach clamored for more than simple nourishment. We could use no animal products whatsoever, so I studied my *Tofu Cookery*, planning banquets of stuffed squash, vanilla tofu pudding, pine nut rice pilaf. I took out my *Moosewoods*, my *Silver Palates*, and chose carrot soup, split pea soup, whole-wheat French bread, West African yam chowder. All these meals existed so vividly in my imagination that before I had even touched a wooden spoon I saw all the retreatants lined up at 11:00, bowls in hand, their eyes bright with expectation.

And, surprisingly, I wasn't far off. I woke at 4:00 every morning and sat in the meditation hall with the group for a half hour, then slipped quietly into the kitchen to start the vats of oatmeal, laced with vanilla and cinnamon. I piled bowls with raisins and almonds, set out cold pitchers of soy milk. My assistant arranged fruit in bowls with the precision and eye of an artist: the oranges gleaming a surreal orange, the apples all showing their good sides, each banana draped at a pleasing angle. I remember pausing outside the kitchen at that hour, in my purple rayon skirt, and seeing the crescent moon dip into the western horizon, clean and sharp as a knife.

I cooked, in those ten days, the way I imagine all truly great cooks do: in a content silence, my attention wholly on the ingredients before me as they assembled themselves into a meal. I chopped onions and garlic, then sautéed them with the dried split peas, added vegetable broth and carrots and celery and fresh thyme. As the soup became soup, the smell of it wafted through the meditation hall, and I could hear people shift a little in their seats, swallow a little more fully in their throats. Later, as I watched them take their bowls to the table, I felt a motherly warmth exude toward all of them, and with a mother's intuition I could feel when the meal hit home. An audible sigh filled the air, a hum of the body satisfied.

When I devoted myself to writing, I felt the same kind of cook's intuition at work, that same heightening of the senses, the oblique and almost random way language accommodated itself to form something new and substantial on the page. So when I decided to write a novel, it didn't surprise me that I chose for my protagonist a woman who worked as a cook. And not just *any* cook, mind you, but a cook who prepares the last meals for inmates on death row. I got the idea after reading a newspaper sidebar about the meals such prisoners request: usually some kind of steak, French fries, southern barbecue. I imagined what it would be like to make such food, to know the meal would be the last taste a person would know on earth.

To complicate the plot, I set the novel in the near future, where many convicts receive the death sentence at the edict of the victims. As a consolation, these condemned receive not only a last meal, but a last smell, sound, touch, and sight. All of these would be orchestrated by my heroine, Willow Dean. She made meals I'm sure have never been ordered on death row: lamb stews with fresh rosemary, Bundt cakes with cardamom, old-fashioned lasagnas served with bottles of dry red wine. The prisoners asked for songs like "Danny Boy," or for a glimpse of their mother's face; they wanted the smell of lilacs just coming into bloom, or the touch of a lover's hand. Willow Dean stood at her stove day after day; she searched out the city for special Italian sausages flecked with fennel, or fresh mozzarella and basil leaves. She sat in the cells with the prisoners as they ate, silent, keeping watch to make sure nothing disturbed them.

The novel tripped all over itself and failed miserably, but the food scenes were all right. Occasionally I still like to get out the manuscript and read those descriptions of the last meals, the prisoners chewing their food so sadly, Willow Dean watching them with a calm and quiet pleasure. And now, whenever I meet someone new—whenever I'm at that delicate threshold between acquaintance and friend—I ask them what they might want for a last meal. I watch as they sit back in their chairs, the rapture that passes over their faces, the distant look in the eyes. I wait, not saying a word, but already I can feel a shift in the air between us. By the time they've leaned toward me again, we've started a friendship that demands nothing less than a good meal to seal it.

My own last meal? It's a complicated proposition. The thought of it is so tied up with all the meals I've read about in my life, all the meals I've imagined but never actually prepared. I think about quail doused in rose petals from *Like Water for Chocolate*, or the trout curling on a platter in a French country inn that M.F.K. Fisher nibbles with such quiet ecstasy. I think about a poem by Li-Young Lee where he recalls a last meal eaten with his father, the slivers of ginger and the drops of sesame oil on the steamed fish in its bamboo cradle. I imagine that elusive steak sandwich I craved so much as a child. I dream my way back into Willie Wonka's chocolate factory, or into Winnie's den, my hands and face slathered in warm honey.

But always, if I'm honest, I come back to that cinnamon toast in the coffee shop at Bullock's Department Store, or to the cinnamon rolls just out of the oven in my mother's kitchen. These foods, I think, would make me happy enough to leave this earth in peace. That, and the fact of my mother sitting so closely beside me, our minds and hearts perfectly in synch. To make the scene exactly right, my mother would read to me as we ate, a book like *Charlotte's Web*, the pages bent open on the table between us. Together, we would eat and read, touching the page and turning, leaving behind our finger-prints, our crumbs, the minutes ticking away, all our persistent hun-gers quelled at last.

Our Daily Toast

Today, for no good reason, I ate two slices of toasted cinnamon/raisin bread at 9:30 A.M., a mere two hours since breakfast. I slathered the first one with whipped butter, and even as I ate it I made up a reason to have another. It was that Ezekiel bread, Biblical, made with pristine sprouted grain, so it couldn't be that bad for you, could it? It might even lead to a brief bout of cinnamon-scented clarity. So I toasted the second one and ate it slowly, slowly, biting off the crust first to leave a perfect round to nibble until I reached the center. The center eaten, and then there was a perfect nothingness—see? Enlightenment. And then a little nap.

Okay, I admit it: I have an unhealthy preoccupation with toast. Do I eat toast socially? Yes. Do I eat toast when alone? Yes. Do I lie about my toast consumption? Yes. Do I hide the evidence of toast consumption? Yes. Do I make up lame excuses for toast consumption? Why yes, yes I do.

My dog loves toast even more than I do, a fact that makes for an ever-ready handy reason to get out the bread sack and fire up the Sunbeam. My dog, contrary to popular belief, can be a little stand-

offish at home, preferring to nap on (or under) my bed, or to disappear altogether upstairs, when her job (clearly laid out to her when
she was hired) is to keep me company at all hours of the day. So,
rather than endure union negotiations, sometimes I resort to bribes
to get her to sit next to me on the couch. Popcorn's always a good
one; as soon as the Redenbacher starts whirring, I can hear Abbe's
feet scrabbling down the stairs, and then her eager face appears in
the doorway to the kitchen. No matter how many times we do this,
she goes into a posture of worship below the kitchen counter, staring
at the popper with such intensity you'd think this billowing cloud of
popped kernels really was a miracle. And as soon as those white drifts
start spilling into the bowl, she jumps up on her hind legs, tail wag-
ging, glances at me wide-eyed, tongue out as if to say: *Do you see this?*
Do you SEE?!

For popcorn, my dog will jump onto the couch and put her head
on my lap, eyes rolled up to watch every blessed movement of hand
to mouth, and I'll feed her a few pieces, one by one. She chomps
every piece with gusto, her lips wide open and smacking, a lusty girl
who loves with abandon. It makes me laugh, this face, and thus I eat
a lot of popcorn. And I watch a lot of TV to justify the popcorn eating, but that's another story altogether.

Toast makes us a little quieter in our devotions. More like communion than a tent revival. More *domestic*. Toast is thoughtful,
whereas popcorn is scattered, hare-brained. Toast is private. After
all, you don't order a bag of toast in the movie theater (though believe me, I would love to!). Toast is something eaten in your pajamas;
toast lends itself to the contemplative perusal of each bite, the way
one's teeth make pretty little scallops in the surface. My dog takes
the bites of crust I offer her delicately, politely, and ducks her head
as she eats them, then looks up and places her nose right in my ear

to say thank you. Abbe and I could eat toast all day and be very happy girls.

It occurs to me that confessing I bribe my dog for love can appear a bit pathetic. It may be just my history of love, a love that even in childhood always felt a bit like barter. You give me this, I'll give you that, and everyone's happy. Toast seems to have always hovered around the edges too: rye toast made from the fresh loaf bought at the Delicious Bakery, my mother calling out, *do you want a piece of toast darling?*, a call that could always bring me back from whatever worlds I had wandered into while playing. I sat placidly at the kitchen table and ate rye toast with butter, keeping my mother company as she put away the rest of the groceries. I kept my eyes on her to see where everything went, on the lookout for Mallomars and Suzie Qs. As I got older, I would make my own toast after arriving home stoned and a little giddy, the toast making the most pleasing crunch in my mouth as I posed at the window, my lips still tender from kisses. I could hear my parents turning out the light in their bedroom, able to sleep now that I was home. The smell of toast meant all their children were safe.

And even later, when I lived with one man and then another and then another, toast could allay even the most bitter arguments. When I lived with Francisco in our mildewed canvas tent at the edge of Lake Powell, we made toast on the iron skillet, a process that required patience and watchfulness and diligence. We spread it with cheap margarine, ate it in silence in the early morning cold. When I lived with Seth at Orr Springs, we made toast on a griddle pan, from loaves we made ourselves, big heavy wheat bread always a little too moist in the middle, studded with hard specks of millet. Toasting made it better, and we spread the slices with homemade apricot jam, made it something to linger over in the mornings before all the chores—wood to be chopped, leaks to be fixed, weeds to be plucked—crowded in to oppress us.

When I lived with Keith, we toasted bread at all hours of the day as we both wrote in our rooms in that little house on Green Lake. He would say, in passing, *This is my life!* and sometimes this cry meant: "I can't believe my good fortune, eating toast with you in this house on the hill!," and sometimes, if the writing weren't going so well, it meant: "I can't believe this is what my life has come to, eating toast with *you* in this house on the hill." But in any case, we enjoyed the toast, made with grainy, slightly sweet bread bought at the co-op down the road. Eating toast made everything good enough, for a little while at least.

For about a year I embarked on a diet that didn't include much bread at all, and one day I realized I hadn't used my toaster in over a month. I put it away, swept off the crumbs that had accumulated underneath, proudly announced on the Weight Watchers message board that I had committed this virtuous act. I got lots of congrats and virtual high-fives, but after a while I looked mournfully at that empty spot on the counter, my dog looked mournfully at me, and I caved. The toaster got trundled out, and I made one Thomas' Light Extra-Fiber English Muffin. Then, a few days later, another. And then a piece of cinnamon toast. On the Weight Watchers board I blamed my dog, but no one bought it. I still lost twenty-five pounds and kept them off, but toasts of all varieties gradually wormed their way back as a daily ritual.

This daily toast doesn't often lead to epiphanies, not of the startling kind, just inaudible sighs, moments of fleeting gladness. Often I hardly notice I'm eating at all, not until my dog puts her paw on my knee, reminds me something momentous is happening: *Look, toast! Do you realize you're eating toast? I could eat some of that toast.* I peel off a bit of crust, the part coated with sesame seeds, and offer it to her just out of reach, so she needs to stretch a little, showing me she wants it enough. She always does, the tip of her snout touching my fingers just for a second, and then her eyes stare into mine, holding me caught in her love as she chews and chews and chews.

Enticement

It is dusk in the field: uncanny, those calls,
the way that voices carry just before the air goes dark.

—ELEANOR WILNER

I

In our yoga class, Alexis starts us off by "doing three Oms together."
We could listen to Alexis all day—a voice that carries the same delicious crackle as her name, a sound like biting into a ripe pear. That
voice coaxes us to do things with our bodies we would never consider
doing on our own. "Breathe in for Om," she says, and we do, our bellies, our chests expanding, then we wait a half-beat for Alexis's voice
to set the pitch—sometimes a deep "ah," sometimes higher, but
never what you think of as that rounded "oh" of Om, never the into-
nation of bearded male yogis in a sonorous chant. No, this seems
more an energetic sigh, or a heraldic call, the hymn of women (we're
all women here), and when we all follow with our own voices to join
with Alexis, it's impossible to know where our own voices end and a
compatriot's begins.

We enter each other this way: our voices expand into a collective oscillation, electric (as if we enact the homonym for Om: "ohm," a unit of electricity, the nanosecond required to create a current of energy). Our small, charged Om keeps expanding—each voice spurring the others—and our throats vibrate, our vocal cords grow supple. We feel—immediately and inexplicably—*filled* with the voices of every woman in the room (I don't mean this as metaphor; it's a physical thing, as if the throat has become nothing but a conduit). Eventually it all closes down in the hum of "Om," and we're quiet in a silence that throbs.

Hannah and Sarah used to do a perfect imitation of Om, either sitting in my meditation room or in the back seat of my car on long road trips with their father. Their small hands bent into perfect *mudras*, thumb and forefinger connected and upright on their knees. They would shut their eyes, their lashes long against their cheeks, and intone "Ommmmm," their necks swooping forward and elongating like cows in a pasture, confusing, perhaps, "moo" and "Om." Or maybe they had it right all along, maybe "moo" and "Om" are more than the palindrome they seem at first glance, those cows making "the sound of everlasting awareness, the ultimate reality, the merging of past, present, and future."

The children, surely, were making fun of me (they couldn't help but crack grins as they mouthed their Oms, their eyebrows raised, their cheeks quivering with pent-up giggles), but they still looked beautiful doing it. I watched them from the front seat, my gaze falling on Hannah first, who sat with remarkably good posture. Her face lost, for a moment, the shy wariness that always marked it and kept me just a body's length away. I shifted my gaze to Sarah, saw her peek at her older sister and then she looked right at me, her face alight with goofiness, always the child ready to be hugged without enticement.

II

In a painting by Ginger Slonaker, a large woman fills the foreground. Seated with a pear in hand, her body looks pear-shaped as well: full at the hips, yellow, ripe. She is the only ripe one in this field: a ghost of a girl hovers at her left knee, and a little bit in the distance, drawn by her gaze, or perhaps by the smell of that pear, two girls approach; they are holding hands but also holding back; still, they find themselves drawn along in the ripples of this landscape, a field brisk with greens, reds, ultramarines. The woman has her head twisted to the side so that we see only her stern profile, her long nose, her mouth set in a line that seems to imply many words that have yet to be said. Or maybe not words, but her own silent "Om": the force of it seems to ripen the entire landscape, even the blue house that stands coolly aflame on a hill in the distance.

I once picked pears with Sarah in a desert orchard. Dawn. We had risen early to catch the light as it animated the sheer red rock cliffs that surrounded us. This orchard was planted by Mormon settlers, and in October the pears ripen as they have done for decades, so we picked them and ate, the flesh just the right balance between yielding and firm, the taste of them so perfectly *pear* that it seemed we ate the platonic ideal of *pear*. It woke us up. We saw deer grazing on the windfall, crossing the creek to get more. Sarah turned to me and said easily, her face swooning with pleasure: "This is the best morning of my life."

The *best*. The *morning*. Our lives together drawing out in a long *Oh* of contentment so simple it had to be true. We had the dawn, we had the red patina of the desert, we had deer, we had our own bodies indulged with pears: what more could there be? Her sister Hannah slept back in the motel, her face pressed into her pillow, but the girls' father cavorted in the field with us, the mouth that once kissed me so fully now so full of pears. We all stood on the bridge and watched the light descend down the rock face until it reached us. "Let's bring some pears to Hannah," Sarah said, gathering them in her shirt. "She's going to be so mad she missed it."

So we gathered pears for Hannah, all of us humming a little tune of love for her, our wish for her to wake.

III

When the Oms die down, we are fully awake. Our bodies still buzz; we still emanate waves, a halation of sound, spreading beyond what first spurred it.

We begin to move our now spacious bodies into downward dog, upward dog, pigeon, cat, and cow: the spine now a flexible thing that can move wherever we desire. While we're in downward dog, Alexis's voice tells us to "look back at your knees," and I can see the other women, upside down, their bodies mirroring my own. "Breathe in," Alexis says, "Heels up. Breathe out, heels down." Her voice is a thread that connects us, and we respond as one body. Up. Down. Plank pose. Extended Child.

In my meditation group at home, we sometimes do a practice called "Second Body." We choose someone from the sangha who will be our second body, and it is for this person we practice. We watch out for her moods, her needs, and give her silent support for her own endeavors. And someone is doing this for us as well, and so we maintain an odd sense that there are now many duplicates of ourselves at work in the world. We don't have to rely on just one. We have an extension of our bodies, slightly larger and more encompassing, dilating in many directions at once.

IV

When I look at Slonaker's painting again, I see that the woman's gaze does not really fall on those girls who slide and hover toward her, rolling on the tide of her own, in-held "Om." No, it's *me* she wants. *See, this pear,* she says, and all of her beckons, entices, though she scares me a little, just like my own grandmother who used to bear down on me with food.

Slonaker's woman has a babushka on her head, like the scarves worn by my ancestors, those women who hummed as they worked. The tail end of this scarf drapes above her shoulder and arcs out to become part of the waves of color that animate the field. The woman's profile, the tail end of her shawl: the two shapes make up in perfect formation the symbol for "Om," a sickle curve painted everywhere in India: on doors of taxis, on market stalls, on the gates of gardens—a kind of spiritual graffiti that reminds everyone who sees it to stop a minute and "contemplate the ultimate." And this woman sits herself in the figure of Om, the pear her mudra, her offering to those bodies that want, and do not want—that are attracted and repelled all at once.

Sarah's father sends me a poem. "A pear sliced," he writes, "resembles soon the inverted heart, skin green, flesh white. . . . I lay them on the plate in cool layers that stick to one another with the glue of juice. They want the former shape, as I do, gravity pulling it back to the whole. . . ."

I thought this painted woman might be enticing the dead to return, but I know now it's really the living that require such ministrations (in whose faces, alas, we see death afoot). When my friend Ruth gave birth to Naomi, we had to lure her out—*come on sweetheart,* we cajoled, *time to be born*—all of us focused on that valley between Ruth's upturned knees. We thought she would never arrive, but now here she is, Naomi, running with her precious balloons across the wood floors of her parents' house, eating baked beans in her high chair, kissing me goodbye when asked.

Or maybe it's the opposite: maybe the dead are the ones who entice us to go on living. At the end of yoga class—after all the sweat, the shaking legs, the hands folded at the heart; after lying in corpse pose for a long time, the mind wandering in and out of the body—we sit up, cross-legged, hands on our knees. "Let's do one more Om to finish," Alexis says, and we breathe in, open our mouths wide, and begin again.

The 23rd Adagio

In May of 1992, a bomb exploded outside a bakery in Sarajevo, killing twenty-two people—Muslims, Croats, Serbs—who had been waiting in line for bread. Each day, for the next twenty-two days, Vedran Smailovic, a cellist with the Sarajevo Opera, put on his black suit; he dragged a chair onto the ruined sidewalk in front of the bakery; he lifted his cello out of its case and played "Adagio en Sol Mineur," by Tomaso Albinoni. A simple piece of music, a sorrowful piece, suited to the cello's frowning countenance. No one asked Smailovic to do this, but each day he closed his eyes and fixed his thoughts on a particular person who had died on that sidewalk. Only when he had this person clearly in mind, would he lift his bow and touch it to the strings. For twenty-two days, he played this music through sniper fire; he played despite artillery shells exploding in the streets; he played as the war in Bosnia escalated around him. He played until the deaths of all twenty-two people had been memorialized by the voice of his solo cello.

When Seattle artist Beliz Brothers heard about Smailovic, she created 22 *Adagio*, a large wall sculpture made of over 100 darkened bread pans hooked together, some holding flowers reminiscent of wilted petals laid on a grave. She displayed the piece for twenty-two days in Seattle in September of 1992, and on each of these days twenty-two cellists played the Adagio in twenty-two different locations around the city. Seattle, for a brief time, was dotted by a music that told a grief most Seattle dwellers could barely comprehend— not only for the twenty-two dead in the bakery bombing, but for the thousands of civilians who died every month as the war continued. Brothers took the sculpture to Washington, D.C., during the Clinton inauguration, and the cellists played for twenty-two days in front of the Red Cross headquarters, the Holocaust museum, the Senate Rotunda—continuing the line of music begun when the Sarajevan cellist picked up his bow.

One day, Smailovic called Brothers on the phone. "Hello, this is Vedran," he said to the stunned artist. He told her he had heard of her work. Brothers told him her sculpture had been chosen as a permanent installation at the Seattle Opera House, and they arranged for Smailovic to fly to Seattle for the dedication of *22 Adagio* on May 24, 1995.

As I drove to Seattle Center for the dedication, I realized another musical event was in town. Clumps of people in tie-dyed shirts ambled down the sidewalks, khaki school buses nosed into full parking lots, girls in long skirts held up signs that read "I need a miracle." The Grateful Dead were playing in Memorial Stadium, next door to the Opera House. In earlier years I would have put on my best swirling skirt and joined the excited crowd surging toward the arena. But on that day I wore chinos and a white t-shirt while I circled lower Queen Anne, just trying to find a parking spot.

By the time I got to the Opera House, a large audience was gathered in the lobby; all the chairs were filled, and groups of people talked together in loud, animated discussion. I pushed through the dense crowd, settled onto the floor, and spied Smailovic across the room: a stocky man with long hair, wearing a black suit with a silver-threaded white scarf draped across his shoulders. No one spoke to him as he leaned on his cello and gazed at 22 *Adagio*.

A security guard in the lobby cracked opened a door just as the first amplified notes of Bob Weir's guitar burst from the stage of Memorial Stadium. I peeked out and could see the yellows and purples of the Grateful Dead crowd already up and bobbing to the beat. The mammoth black speakers stood no more than a hundred yards away, and the opening song picked up speed and volume, the bass booming against the walls, Jerry Garcia warbling in his seductive way to the crowd.

A collective gasp of amused protest, surprise, and apprehension rose from the audience in the lobby. We looked at each other and shrugged, good sports, but surely we wouldn't be able to hear Smailovic clearly, we wouldn't be able to appreciate his passionate bowing, we wouldn't experience this music in its purity. The door quickly closed, but the Grateful Dead remained a presence in the room, hardly muted, the beat driving hard for dancing, the words of the songs loud and clear. People shook their heads. "Too bad," someone murmured. "Poor planning," I heard someone reply.

But a remarkable thing happened when Smailovic sat down in the center of the lobby, cello gripped lightly in his left hand, the bow in his right. The cellist closed his eyes, and suddenly he was gone from us, a shadow of deep grief falling across his face. "Touch of Grey" blasted through the walls, but Smailovic seemed oblivious to the music, oblivious to the fact that he was in America, incognizant of his audience of well-wishers and sympathizers. Behind him, an enlarged black-and-white photograph showed Smailovic in Sarajevo, his arm crooked around his cello, one hand covering his eyes. Now, here in Seattle, Smailovic sat in front of that bakery again, the rubble all around him, sniper bullets whizzing through the air. He carried the war with him, tangible as the smell of smoke on a person's clothes, or a stain of blood on a shirt.

Before sitting down, Smailovic had told us the war in Bosnia is "not a civil war, but a war against civilians. Three hundred thousand of my countrymen have died. This is a massacre, not a war." Turning to the sculpture he said, "A twenty-third person died in hospital many weeks after the bombing. So tonight we will play the 23rd Adagio."

Eyes still closed, Smailovic leaned forward and drew his bow across the strings, the high notes soft at first, barely audible, then gradually descending in scale, the bow pulled a little more forcefully across the instrument. The voice of the cello expanded in gradual increments, the line of the melody asserting itself, a little louder, a little louder, until finally the piece crescendoed—and the single cello, played by a single man, completely drowned out the amplified rocking of the band next door. Smailovic kept his eyes closed, and he played the "Adagio en Sol Mineur" for the twenty-third victim of the bakery bombing; he played for the 300 thousand dead, for the Muslim women raped in concentration camps, for the children of these rapes left in orphanages across the country. The cello, so loud the music completely enveloped even those sitting far back, became the undaunted voice of Smailovic's rage and sorrow.

When Smailovic played in front of the bakery in Sarajevo, he did not wait for the noise of the war to die down; he did no planning to ensure he would be heard "correctly." As the piece descended from its climax, the strains of the Grateful Dead merged back into the room, so that for a moment the two musics played against one another, within one another, moving together in uneasy balance. Here, as in Sarajevo, Smailovic's cello was not isolated or rarefied, heard only in the controlled setting of the auditorium, all unwanted noises filtered out. In his homeland, his music emanated from the center of the chaos, meshed with it, cried out a message in direct contradiction to the war as it happened all around him.

Smailovic lifted his bow off the strings and held it upright as the vibration of the Adagio faded away. You can't wait, sometimes, for the setting to be perfect, he seemed to tell us in his silence. You have to make yourself heard, even if it's just for a moment or two, when the music takes on a life of its own and leaves the shelter of your hands.

Secret Machine

My loneliness is a secret machine,
a flying featherbed in the blue
of a hydrangea.

—CHRISTOPHER HOWELL

I

In Tara Parson's prints, airplanes fly at you from many angles: sometimes head on, emerging from a far corner of the sky, or buzzing away, swooping straight into the stratosphere. Sometimes they tilt a bit, as if nodding their wings in your direction, and sometimes they seem to startle back, rearing above an inexplicable black plume. Most often they stay a course away from the center, grazing the edge—a nimbus of white wings and tail, a sleek, empty body that punctuates otherwise deep fields of blue. At first glance this blue seems harmless, and the planes themselves oddly cheerful, like stenciled decorations adorning the room of a beloved child, one who wakes happy and calls out for his mother—not in distress, no, but wanting only to share his glee at the airplanes that greet him.

Tara works all day in her studio, and sometimes at night, cautiously blading the stencils of the same airplane—a toy model of a Continental Airlines jet—and then pulling them through the press to see how they will fly. Sometimes you feel the uplift, and sometimes the breath-catch of touchdown (the pilot's voice through the static, calm, but remote: *Okay folks, we're beginning our final descent*), but most often you're reminded of that pause in the middle of the long flight, a stretch of time when the plane settles in; you feel suspended in that blue, with no clear destination, and you think maybe you'll be up here forever: reading your book, doing the crossword, dozing, waiting for the rattle of the in-flight service cart making its second rounds.

When you see these prints in Tara's studio, hanging from a line by clothespins, you can get a little dizzy: this multitude of jets inching forward inexorably, both in motion and deathly still. And you try not to notice that some of these planes spiral down the page, leaving ghost images behind. Sometimes her prints, Tara tells me, are altered by accident, a slight shift that happens as she makes the hard crank of the press wheel, and what emerges from that plate comes as a surprise, no matter how carefully she's cut out the stencils or applied the wide swathes of ink.

There's something about them that makes you uneasy, these passenger jets and their invisible cargo: they threaten to creep out the corner of the frame if we glance away, and then where will we be? With only that sky to seize us? A famous sculptor comes to Tara's studio, and turns to each wall, the prints hanging in their gentle rows, all those planes flying, and says, *Is this about 9/11?* And his question is wary, as if to say, *because if they're all about 9/11, then I don't want to know*. So how can Tara answer?

She turns the wheel of the press and another print emerges, the blue unpredictable, volatile. *I started working on these images out of fear*, she says. It's hot in the studio, and the stenciled planes are precise, and sometimes she has to keep cutting new ones because ink stains them, they get a little bloodied, and so they're no good anymore, they'd ruin the effect. And so she has to keep cutting, hunched over on her stool, the Exacto knife quite exact, exacting.

The famous sculptor says Tara must not start loving her planes too much, or else they will become too pretty, and we *don't like pretty*; no, we need that edge to make it beautiful, that little bit of *antagonie*, the pull between two opposing forces—the will to live, the lure of death—to make the image hold fast and not disintegrate, the way planes are wont to do, the way any solid thing heaved up in the air will naturally incline to fall. *Okay folks*, the pilot says, so calm in the face of it, *we're beginning our final descent.*

II

My friend Eden is afraid of flying. Whenever she boards a plane, she concentrates very hard on keeping the craft in air. *We all have to think good thoughts*, she says, shooting glances at her fellow passengers, but most of them seem oblivious, arguing with the stewardess, or with a child, or just tuning out altogether, sleeping with their heads thrown back, their mouths open in horrible, wide Os, as if already struck dead. So she does it herself, thinking, *The plane will fly, the plane will fly*, like an old woman at her rosary, until the stewardesses come by and tap the seats to bring them back to a full upright position.

Tara turns the wheel again, and again. I think of her there in the dim space of the press room, and the prints accumulate, the planes leaving the hangar and taking flight: each one circumscribed by prayer, the slightest touch, but enough to keep them flying. She becomes, through this ceaseless attention, her namesake: the Tibetan deity Tara, a goddess who, for Buddhists, lives as a guardian. This Tara manifests in multiple, colored forms: Green Tara, for action; White Tara, of the mind; Yellow Tara, of wealth; Red Tara, for joy; and, most holy, Blue Tara for protection. Blue Tara, according to scripture, is "the remover of obstacles." She "teaches us to transform the distorted energy of wrath and anger into the wisdom of clarity."

Tara's blue prints emerge from the roller, each one different, but each one holding steady, those planes in a holding pattern. *What I'm trying to get at*, Tara says, *is the moment just before the next thing will happen. . . .* And she tells us later, her face disintegrating: *I lost my best friend in 9/11, why can't I just say it?*

Because it's unspeakable. So she rewinds time and the planes do not make their terrible turns, those cuts in the blue air. She is printing her monotypes, saying her rosary, she is dancing the Dance of Twenty-one Taras; she keeps turning the wheel, that Tibetan prayer wheel, the groaning revolutions you see on the high ridges of the Himalayas, spinning out a continual *Om Mani Padme Huhm* into the changed air.

She hangs them with clothespins—they bend the line in a slight curve—and so the prints become prayer flags, those fluttering cloths, edges frayed, that you see strung on high ridges in Tibet, or swooping down from the temple peaks. You can buy them yourself at the little hippie shop on Main, string them in your backyard to border a garden, or hang them inside to animate empty thresholds between rooms. These flags waft continuous prayers into the air—prayers for protection, prayers for peace. Sometimes it's the Wind Horse flying among the calligraphy, but most often Tara's image stamps the rough cloth, again and again: duplicates of one woman guarding the skies.

III

I have always believed in a vertical purity. . . .

There's a moment in the first movement of Beethoven's violin concerto: the orchestra has been beating a careful pulse beneath the soloist's violin—a viola plucked here and there, a steady percussive in the background—and then suddenly, without your knowing it, the orchestra has vanished and the violin soars out there by itself, light-headed in space. It floats untethered—no, not floating but flailing upward, into the stratosphere, trying to reiterate melodies the orchestra has already negotiated, but the air's too thin, it won't quite make it; the violinist tries though, tries so hard, and in this striving cuts a path through your brain, stenciling its own shape: a sharp triangle of wing.

And if you listen to this music carefully—if you set aside everything else and just listen, eyes closed, hands at rest in your lap—you'll feel that violin right behind your eyes, the place where a pool of lamentation abides, before specific tears shape themselves for a specific grief. And just when you think the violin will have to quit, to clatter broken-stringed to the ground, a viola edges back in to help: plucking, sidling up the way you might approach someone in pain, unsure if she really wants help and so you just hold out your hands to see if she'll grab on. . . .

And she does. Well, it's rather like that: the violin falls back into the orchestra's arms, and takes up the song in full force, all of them together and rejoicing at being together again, unharmed, laughing even at the way the violin got lost there for a minute. And you, the bystander: you can breathe again.

. . . and the air steps back from each body in song. . . .

IV

The prayer flags keep waving, a zephyr of praise that keeps the world's grief cooled. And I think of Galileo, his theory of falling bodies, how predictable it is now: the time it takes any two people to land. And Tara keeps printing her monotypes, untitled, the isolated planes never touching down. *The moment before the next thing.* . . . Not the impact, not the inward swooping we've already seen—again and again—because we couldn't stop watching, even when we clicked off our televisions and went to wash the dishes and walked the dog, those planes kept crashing; as soon as our grief ebbed, we watched the planes again, as if by watching we might somehow make amends.

> . . . *the sky a pale plate*
> *of nothingness—nothingness—*
> *then the cirrus-cloud tails*
> *rushing through.*

Tara delays the planes, rather like the trains of De Chirico, paralyzed by *the enigma of the hour,* halted, yet moving; never arriving, never departing; keeping company with the dead who don't yet know they're deceased. She is not a painter of still lifes, not an artist who would place nice figurines just so on a wrinkled cloth: statuettes of Mother Mary, perhaps, or Kuan Yin, two saints who keep their heads tilted to the side, just so, their faces ripe with compassion for those who suffer. But her monotypes are still lifes of a sort: the one plane flying still through her life. *Memento Mori.* Stalled Life. The plane stalled overhead. As if it, too, could feel a premonition and rear back, try to keep at bay whatever will happen next.

And never happens next. Not here. Not now. But grief, too, can be a secret machine that keeps humming long after you've clicked off the engine, shut the door on it, walked away. You sit in the kitchen, drinking coffee and passing the time, thinking how to decorate your rooms, those empty thresholds beckoning. Maybe you listen to Beethoven and swoop your arms through the air, a maestro conducting by proxy such music. Or perhaps you'll watch the prayer flags wave in the garden, flapping their good wishes to whoever passes by. But that engine keeps purring. And eventually those planes might spin back into toys, clutched in the hands of a child who loves them.

*The italicized lines of poems throughout sections III and IV are lifted from "The Ghost Trio," by Linda Bierds.

Opalescent

I

I'm buying stained-glass panels for the windows of my new home. They're from a store called Rejuvenation in Portland, and my friend Kathleen has encouraged me to get them. She now sits in one of the lush, reupholstered chairs in the showroom, her hands clasped in her lap, her head tilted just a little to the side as she watches me, bemused at the gravity I've lent to this endeavor.

Rejuvenation has many, many Tiffany-inspired glass panels from which to choose: There are floor-to-ceiling windows all along the back wall—enormous paintings of climbing morning glory or gingko trees—and lamps with clusters of glass that bend into dangling wisteria or the sleek bodies of dragonflies. I don't live in Portland, so to make a choice now is full of risk—what if I don't like the window once I get it home? What if it cracks on the way?—but now that the longing to buy has transmuted into the inevitable purchase, there's no turning back.

I keep returning to a triptych that hangs vertically in a side window: a white lotus flower blossoming up top, with vines that

211

interweave and flow down three sections to reach, finally, an unopened bud. The glass winks in shades of lavender and teal. I pay the $250, and a nice salesman wraps it up securely in layers of cardboard for me take back to Bellingham. Later, Kathleen kisses me goodbye, sorrow and joy consorting on her face to make it strangely alight. All the way home, I'm aware of the stained glass in its box beside me: a container of pent-up brilliance, already broken, put back together again.

II

Marc Chagall: *For me a church window represents the transparent partition between my heart and the heart of the world.*

I first saw Chagall stained glass at the Art Institute of Chicago. You see the light before you actually see the windows: a lavender glow as you come down the stairs into the foyer of the museum. I stood with my friend Kristin before *American Windows*, glass collages that incorporate classic Chagall motifs: figures floating midair or perched improbably in the crowns of trees; birds soaring in currents of yellow and red; objects unhinged from any force that once kept them aligned. All of it seems a frenetic act of worship, the faces drawn upward, offering candles and song.

Kristin and I stood there together, transfixed in the Chagall blue. Glass, perhaps, afforded Chagall his perfect medium, though he came to it late, well past the age of seventy. Chagall, whose paintings emerge from his Judaism ("Were I not a Jew," he said, "I would not have become an artist"), first assembled a stained glass mosaic for a Catholic church—the Church of Notre Dame de Toute Grace—in France. He considered it a privilege to create windows for holy places. He took no payment for his work.

Kristin walked on, anxious, I think, to get to the O'Keeffes. A doctoral student at the University of Chicago, studying comparative theologies, Kristin will eventually travel to southern India, squatting in huts and asking Hindu women, in her rudimentary Tamil, about their reverence for the Virgin Mary.

As far as I know, Chagall did not piece together the Virgin in cobalt blue glass, her head tilted to the side in compassion, but if he had I imagine she would look much like the primary model for his paintings, his first wife Bella, her skin a pallor that turns incandescent under her husband's brush. Bella's head, in both photographs and paintings, tilts to the side the way Mary's does, a half-smile tugging at her lips.

Bella died in 1944. She and her husband had been married almost thirty years. For nine months Chagall's brush lay still and quiet in his studio. I wonder how the light felt to him then, if the windows clouded over and became opaque. He had not yet discovered stained glass as a vehicle, but maybe that's what he needed— scythes of blue, eruptions of yellow—and the deliberate, tender restoration of all that can be lost.

III

Ann Gardner, an artist who lives in Bellingham, is known for mosaic sculptures that mimic waves upon waves of unsettled water. She got her start in mosaic when commissioned to create a tile wall on a stairway in Seattle. "I made all the tiles," she said, "And I laid them all down and there just wasn't enough energy for me. So I took a hammer and broke them all."

IV

Down in California, my friends Rhea and Jim are building a patio. They use what they call "rip-rap": chunks of concrete ripped out of houses undergoing restoration. They pick it up in town when they hear of it on the local radio station: people have extra rip-rap to give away, and you haul it back home yourself. They finished about half the patio when they ran out of rip-rap, and the truck used to haul it had broken down, exhausted under the weight.

What to do? After a few days of gazing with yearning at their unfinished patio, they simply decided to make their own.

So they created a mold, poured cement and aggregate into it, let it dry, then went at it with sledgehammers. They broke it into pieces—they broke it apart—merely to put it back together again with the barest of spaces between the fragments. We both laugh as Rhea tells me about this process, how silly it seems when you actually do it: to create something whole, only to destroy it, to have those pulverized pieces come together again to mimic the whole.

As we stand on the completed patio, I see they have planted small, tender starts of creeping thyme to fill in these spaces with greenery and fragrance. It's the kind of herb that can be trampled; in fact it likes foot traffic and will thrive there, filling in the cracks the way lead does on stained glass, or mortar in mosaics. Up the hill they've planted a perennial garden, mulched against the summer heat by a layer of cocoa husks so that now, in the late June sun, the garden smells of chocolate, wafting across us where we stand on the broken ground.

V

I was a child in love with jigsaw puzzles, starting slowly with the big-eyed puppies and clowns, moving on to the 100-piece, then 500, then inevitably 1000-piece contraptions. Where did we do them? I think my father must have built us a special puzzle tray, a flat board we lifted from the kitchen table at mealtime, replaced a little later, after dessert. I can see his high cheekbones and the dimples I've inherited, the five o'clock shadow lining his face. Of course, like all good puzzlers, we created as much of the border as we could first, then filled the interior at a slow, methodical pace that required patience. You need to be willing to try, and fail, and try again—nudging the contours of the pieces together, sometimes roughly, sometimes softly, always the snap/sigh combination when the piece hits home.

Often we kept the television on, or the radio, and we must have been serenaded by the sound of my mother washing the dishes and scrubbing her stove. We must have looked up from our work occasionally, watched a bit of the show, said something to my mother; my brothers must have joined us now and then, never sitting but hovering, reaching out their basketball-grimed fingers to shove a piece in. But I prefer to remember father and daughter at this shared task of assemblage alone, the only sound the muted scuff of puzzle pieces across the board, an occasional sigh, and the crisp tap when a piece settled into place.

I imagine us at this for hours, the day outside our suburban window draining away, the new landscape unfolding before us bit by bit (vistas we would never see in real life: baronial white mansions, spreading seas of lavender, wooden bridges across leaf-strewn streams). At first we used the box cover, propped up, as a guide. But after a

while we glanced up at it less often, training our eyes to see by intuition, to feel our way toward the center piece by piece, color by color,
through instinct alone.

Sometimes I liked the completed puzzle so much my father would
spray it with a special adhesive and hang it up on my bedroom wall.
I'd gaze at the picture admiringly for a few weeks or so, but after
awhile the glow of accomplishment faded, and the picture turned
tawdry, dull, a fake. The point was never the picture after all. What
I loved (I knew even then) was the process of *rememberment*. As if
the picture were itself a dim memory, a collective loss, and through
our grave attention we brought it to life again.

VI

I've never broken a bone in my life. I say this sentence more often than
I would think necessary, and I say it with obvious pride, as if to keep
my bones intact this long is some sort of accomplishment. Not for me
the heavy cast on the arm, dirtied on the playground, adorned with
spirals and flowers of magic marker. But the first boy I kissed had a
broken wrist, and his cast lay inert on his lap as we sought out each
other's mouths. His breath smelled of alfalfa sprouts, or maybe that
was the rancid odor emanating from thick plaster and gauze. My
hand, I vaguely remember, fell to rest on his cast, and I think, knowing me, that I stroked it gently, as if it really were just an extension
of his knobby wrist.

Bones, after all, are used to it. Even in good health, they're always
in the process of breaking. Every minute the osteoclasts gnaw away
at the old collagen, and the osteoblasts muscle in to lay down fresh
cells. When a bone breaks, the stem cells begin a mad dash, speeding
up their rate of duplication a thousand-fold. The osteoblasts speed up

too, laying down the collagen, the minerals, the calcium, until you have a whole bone, *good as new.*

Because of this cycle, any human bone is never more than 20 years old. Look at your arm, beyond the skin to divine the ulna and radius— no longer "hard as bone" but always in a state of flux, neither ruined nor repaired, but somewhere in between. Or place your chin in your hand, feel that jawbone: how solid it seems! How wholly your own bone, that's been with you a thousand years, jawing through conversations both mundane and profound, meals that left you swooning.

But really that bone's barely older than an adolescent, just now reaching her prime. That other bone—the one that had your first kiss, the one that felt the stroke of the first man you really loved—it's gone, dissolved. Where does that leave us, with all these naive bones? Have they learned a thing?

Don't grieve. Think of it as *rejuvenation*.

VII

And you see where this leads:

> The foot bone connected to the . . . leg bone,
> The leg bone connected to the . . . knee bone,
> The knee bone connected to the . . . thigh bone . . .
> Oh hear the word of the Lord!

And so on. Actually what Ezekiel said was: "and behold, there were very many in the open valley, and lo, they were very dry. And he said unto me, Son of Man, can these bones live? . . . and there was a noise, and behold a shaking, and the bones came together, bone to his bone. . . ."

VIII

. . . So I took a hammer and broke them all . . .

Sometimes the stained glass catches my eye by surprise. I forget, but not for long, that these pieces glisten in my window, submissive to whatever light happens on them.

Louis Comfort Tiffany grew famous for his memorial windows: commissions made by grieving families to remember the dead. A highly private man, yet gregarious, he threw lavish costume balls and built an entire estate, Laurelton Hall, as a testament to his art. He invented opalescent window glass, a process whereby color fuses into the glass itself, creating a rich texture impossible to obtain by mere application. He was, as some critics suggest, "intoxicated with color."

And so when asked to create memorial windows to be set in the walls of churches, a standard practice in the late nineteenth century, Tiffany balked at the convention of biblical scenes and veered instead into landscapes lush with color and light. The church frowned on this, but the families loved it: in one of his most famous memorial windows, *Magnolias and Irises* (ca. 1908), a field of purple iris leads the eye to a luminescent pool fed by a river snaking through the overlapping hills in the background. The water, a recurrent motif in the memorial windows, represents the River of Life, bearing departed souls from this realm to the next. Above it all, a stand of magnolia trees bursts into full bloom, echoing the golds and pinks of sunrise.

Bishop Durande de Mende: *Stained glass windows are divine writings that spread the clarity of the true sun, who is God, through the heart of the faithful, bringing them true enlightenment.*

IX

Rhea has joined a quilting circle. The women sit together once a month with their squares spread out on their laps, stitching and talking through the rainy winter months. None of them really knew how to quilt at first; they learned the craft together, bit by bit, and soon the quilting became a back rhythm to their conversations, allowed their thoughts free reign.

Rhea came to visit me when I moved into my new house, before the furniture was in place, the windows still unadorned. She brought with her some squares she was piecing together from scraps of blue silk, a bit of gold. She sat on my front lawn while I tinkered with my new potted plants. Rhea made each stitch carefully, the needle appearing and disappearing among the weave of the cloth.

Two Jehovah's Witnesses came by—in their stiff suits and sickly smiles—and asked us if we worried about where our souls would go when we die. Rhea just kept stitching her squares, and without looking up murmured that she had no worries at all. She said it with such conviction—no worries *at all*—the witnesses turned away without argument and headed for the next house. I heard my 90-year-old neighbor open the door, and her quavery voice as she answered them: "Well, I prefer not to think too much about it."

When I hold Rhea's quilt, or run my hand along its surface (this instinctive gesture when confronted with such broken and re-assembled things), it's as though I touch an essential body that lies just beneath the coverlet of skin (*them bones, them bones, them dry bones* . . .). And I sense not only my friend's presence in the quilt, but all the women who spoke as they sat together commiserating: a rough man, a troublesome child, the drought, the flood—all these voices dissolved in the space between each stitch.

As Roethke put it: "May my silences become more accurate."

X

My friend Suzanne once broke her wrist and wore a cast for several weeks up to her elbow. The day they sawed through the plaster, the technicians split away the two sides to reveal a hand transformed: a thick mat of dark hair covered the back of her hand, *like an animal's coat*, she says, laughing. *I looked like a freak*. She finally went back to her doctor, to see what had happened. He told her it was normal, to be expected. When a bone breaks, growth hormones flood the area, eager to repair but unable to distinguish exactly which kinds of growth to facilitate. I imagine these hormones like a mass of children let loose for recess after a long day of rain, their energy so effervescent they swarm over anything in their path. They urge everything to flourish. *Grow, grow!* they shout. *Mend!*

XI

As stained glass artistry grew, the lead lines that were once accepted as a necessary and decorative element became necessary evils to be camouflaged by the design. . . .

When Chagall made his now famous "Jerusalem Windows," he saw them as "jewels of translucent fire." His windows have been described by art historians as "jewel-hard and foamy, reverberating and penetrating, radiating light from an unknown interior." Chagall, himself, in a summation of his life's work said: "My art is an extravagant art, a flaming vermilion, a blue soul flooding over my paintings."

XII

They call it "Chartres blue." In the miles of stained glass that bejewel Chartres Cathedral—an hour's train ride from Paris—a violet-blue light emanates that no one had really encountered before the 12th century. Can you imagine it? A pilgrim, you trudge up the hill toward the bristling spires, each tower etched with hundreds of saints who wink and smile in the muted light. You enter the nave with its cobbled labyrinth, and you sink to your knees, crawling toward salvation along these winding paths. The only light in the immense dark beams steadily from the stained glass, and it is enough, more than enough. Everywhere you turn there is more of it, up high and down low, the rose windows presiding over the portals. The blue—a color so new to your eyes that your mind ceases its babble, speechless—accumulates pane by pane, until it bathes your retinas in the glow of the saved.

Or imagine this: You are a worker, a tradesman, in the twentieth century, a time of what they call the "great" wars. You live in the village of Chartres, and everyone knows what's coming. You climb up scaffolds and begin removing the stained glass windows, painstakingly, bit by bit, so they won't be destroyed by errant bombs—all of Europe now quaking, and it's up to you to save what can be saved. It doesn't matter how much time it takes. Each piece comes away easily once you've loosed it from its lead casing, and you label it, put it in its proper box. A new kind of light streams into the cathedral, naked and unadorned. Who can be saved in such a glare? Once the war is over, once a peace is certain, you will climb once again and replace the windows, bit by bit. Maybe they won't be finished before you die—such a restoration might take decades, the slow time necessary for such consecrated light to return. But you persevere, fitting each piece of stained glass into its socket, until finally the litany of saints might be whole again.

XIII

My friend Kristin has returned from India. When she answers the phone, we coo to each other a few moments of our pleasure—her voice finally in my ear after so many long months, my voice in hers. I'm slouched on my sofa looking at, but not really seeing, my new stained glass windows from Rejuvenation; she's in her new apartment in Chicago, two roommates hovering somewhere out of sight.

She tells me about a temple in India with its twenty-two sacred wells. She tells me about walking through this temple and undergoing a strange baptism: at each well the guide poured buckets of water over their heads, three times each—so, sixty-six dunkings in the course of an hour. "It was bizarre," she says, "but also. . . ." We pause for a moment, the line that connects us suspended.

"Afterward I had to lie outside in the garden, I was so tired. I fell asleep, all these people around me and I'm sleeping like a baby."

And while she talks I imagine the Chagall blue, the Chartres blue: Kristin with her blue eyes, in her blue sari, her leather sandals, the whisper of her footsteps in the halls, the splash of water over her head. She tells me about the worn stone floors, the puddled water from the pilgrims that came before, light flickering along the dim temple walls. Though the rest of India glares on the plain, inside this temple my friend is baptized again and again, drenched in holy water, calm and cool, wholly herself.

XIV

I make my own pilgrimage to see it: the Chartres blue. And even on the train I felt a slight shift in my mood, an expansion of the self out of its narrow channel of worry and preoccupation. For days I'd been wandering, checking museums off the list, hopping on and off the Metro like an expert, pretending to have a good time. But I've been recovering from a broken heart, and so the City of Light has been tainted a bit, and I found myself irritably glancing at lovers along the Seine, impatiently shouldering by them to get another helping of Berthillion sorbet. There's too much light in Paris, the days reaching 90 degrees and the sun setting at 10 P.M., until sometimes I just want it all to go dark.

But on the train to Chartres, and in the cathedral itself, I get it: the divine balance of light and dark, the heat tempered by the centuries' old stone. There's a noonday mass going on in the central sanctum, the priest's slow voice amplified so that it seems to start nowhere, to emerge from the air itself. There are only a few people actually participating in the mass, the rest of us circling around them as we keep our heads tilted toward the massive windows that loom at every turn.

I light a votive candle in front of a Mary carved from pear wood; she's holding high the infant Jesus in her arms. It's said that children came here during "troubled times" and prayed to Mary for her comfort and guidance. I stand there in front of my sputtering candle, my hands held like a lotus against my chest, and whisper the only prayer I really know these days: the *metta* prayer of Buddhism, wishing for all beings to be free from fear. Because right at this moment—in a place that has weathered so much history, and that has absorbed so many supplications—I'm thinking fear must be the root of all of it, all our suffering. And all our prayers merely aimed at a dissolution of that fear into something akin to a mother's hush.

Afterward I walk down the center aisle, and though most of the ancient labyrinth is cluttered with chairs, I place my feet carefully on the smooth cobbles of the exposed bits of the path, weaving my way in an odd, sideways little dance.

XV

From photographer André Kertész: *We can never know how beautiful nature is. We can only guess.*

And perhaps that's what Tiffany was up to, with his stained glass: taking wild stabs at it. I imagine him walking the grounds of Laurelton Hall, pausing in the courtyard to admire his fountain: an octagonal pool trimmed with iridescent glass, an elegant, favrile vase rising from the center . . . *and as the light fell on it the colors glimmered like mother-of-pearl.* . . . I imagine him passing his fountain and stopping for a moment under the magnolia tree, the heavy wisteria. *We can never know how beautiful nature is. We can only guess.*

These days, when I walk to work, I'm often confronted by the locust trees in front of Old Main, just now coming into their yellow fever. It's all uphill, this walk, and so each tree comes into view incrementally: I see the crown, then the low branches, then the weathered trunk. And my eyes perceive the broken pieces rather than the whole: I see each leaf as the individual fragment of the tree itself. And at the same time, no leaf exists in isolation: the single leaf would not carry the aspect of the season as much as this multiplicity of leaves, all of them conjoining in this singular pattern we think of as *autumn* or *locust* or *tree*.

The trees are losing their leaves, of course they are. It is not unexpected; we saw it coming all along. The leaves fall along the brick pathways, obscuring the proper way. Some of the people I pass notice this disassembling, but most do not. Some of the leaves fly up and whirl out of our way. Some of them, but not all, disintegrate under our feet.

  . . . *a transparent partition, between my heart and the heart of the world.* . . .

In any case, we walk easily, without fear, each of us held together by camouflaged ribbons of bone.

The Dog at the Edge of the World

I've been looking for one of my favorite Franz Marc paintings called *The Dog at the End of the World*. At least I *think* that's what it's called; I had the image on a postcard I gave away, and I've never been able to find it again—not online, not in an art shop, not in my book of Marc paintings. I gave away this card to a man I'd been dating only a short time. I gave it to him because he had an unruly dog he seemed to love despite her flaws, and I tried to love her so he would love me. But that dog was incorrigible, a thin black lab so excited by any glance of attention that she jumped on laps, peed on floors, turned herself inside out in her devotions. None of it worked, not her pleas for love, not my own dog-as-cupid matchmaking, this love by proxy. Shortly thereafter, the man broke up with me—in a way that was so passive-aggressive I didn't quite realize I'd been dumped, and so I kept calling, left messages that rose with a question mark at the end—and so I've never seen my Dog at the End of the World again.

Now, years later, I don't want the man back, but I do want this postcard, my dog at the end of the world. Maybe she was called the

Dog at the *Edge* of the World. Either way, I remember her as a small white dog, sitting with her back to the viewer, dwarfed by a vista that stretches out vast and light and covered in snow. This dog does not seem dismayed to be at the edge of such blankness, such unknowns, nor does she seem eager to go out into it, to tip over that edge and explore. No, the dog is merely—as my remembered title suggests— simply *at* the edge, content to be in the space between the known and the unknown. I think she even rests her head on her forepaws, eyes half-closed in contentment.

Maybe this picture doesn't even really exist. Perhaps I've con- flated several different Franz Marc paintings to create this one, reso- nant image of a dog immersed in a landscape broken into Marc's characteristic shards. Marc painted animals of all sorts: cows, chick- ens, deer, cats; dogs are by no means his favorite totem. In another painting, *Deer in the Monastery* (this one I can find with no problem), he paints the faint outlines of one resting deer emerging from swaths of green, resplendent in a single ray of light. The deer looks so rest- ful, so at peace, her head tilted up, bathed in the last rays of sun that find her here, deep in a garden tended by the careful hands of monks. I imagine she's a fawn, with faint polka dots of infancy just fading into the tawny fur, the skin taut, not yet pitted by age. She rests, legs folded, accompanied by a chorus of strange birds who, until this moment, have not known how to burst into song.

Perhaps I've fixated on the dog at the edge of the world because I'm just now beginning to understand what Winston Churchill called the "black dog" of depression. *This* animal, I know now, has been at my heels for years, an unstinting companion. Perhaps I see Marc's white dog as a kind of redemption, how she sits so restfully on the dangerous precipice. And I want to grab that animal back from my fickle lover's hand, have this white dog returned to me: this animal he couldn't have really understood or loved the way she deserves.

As it turns out, Marc himself suffered from severe anxiety and depression. He escaped on the night of his first marriage in the throes of an anxiety attack that would lead him to Paris, into the sanctuary of the paintings of Van Gogh, Cezanne, and Gauguin. His anxiety, as he put it, "numbed the senses," and he came back to his senses through studying those artists who amplified the world, made it brighter, more intense. These artists studied the natural world, knew it intimately, and through this intimacy could carry out acts of profound transformation. In one of his letters, Marc writes: "I am trying to intensify my feeling for the organic rhythm of all things, to achieve pantheistic empathy with the throbbing and flowing of nature's bloodstream in trees, in animals, in the air."

Marc found his subject in animals, and he became an expert through careful observation. He kept himself afloat by teaching animal anatomy classes in his Paris studio, showing others how an animal's body can only be depicted in abstraction once you thoroughly understand the primary reality of muscle and bone. His animals gradually transformed from realistic renderings to the faintest suggestion of animal forms emerging from a chaos of color.

I stare at one of his more famous paintings, *The White Dog* (this image you can find everywhere): a sleek white dog, asleep in a patch of snow, so it becomes a study in repose, in calm. The dog gradually merges into the landscape—the white fur, the white back, echoing the white of the snow. It's a close-up, the rest of the world cut out of the frame so that our eyes fill only with sleeping dog, a dog who must be inured to the cold. I briefly wonder if this is my white dog, just so my search can be over, but something about the animal isn't quite right. I think *my* white dog must be more complex—both afraid and content, holding many opposing emotions at once—while this white dog has found his place too easily, can lie down in the snow and think nothing of it.

And now, through another brief foray of Internet circumnavigation, I've found it, my white dog. But it turns out not to be a dog at the end of the world, nor a dog at the edge of the world, but a *Hound Before the World*. A hound, and he looks it, much bigger than I remember, squatting on his large haunches, ribs clearly visible in his barrel torso, bulbous forelegs muscular as a weightlifter's. His ears droop down to either side of his jowly face, and his black eyes look out onto the world with an expression I can't quite articulate: certainly not the calm I remembered, more like bewilderment. Before I found the painting again, my dog was just a pinpoint on the horizon, but now here he is, large as the world, which shatters in pieces of blue and red and yellow and orange, not monochromatic at all.

I don't know what to do with him, this hound. He's too big, too goofy, too . . . how do I put it . . . too *male*. He doesn't know or understand that he's a dog at the edge or the end of the world; rather he's *before* it, a stance that, to me, feels completely different. He's paused momentarily between past and future; he's not invested in what lies across that divide. He's got a master, no doubt. He's got someone who's about to call him back, throw him a bone, bring him home.

I want my own white dog back—the one I fabricated, the one who led me to the edge and allowed me to sit still, showed me how to be alone with no need to either leap into the abyss or back away. The pill I take now to help me navigate depression really does the same thing: it helps me to see how to stay a little bit longer at the edge and observe—often with bemusement rather than despair. After years of yoga, meditation, therapy—things that helped, but never seemed to really take root—I'm finally able to sidle up to the viewpoint and begin to enjoy the view. Like a tourist lured by a roadside attraction, I stop to read the interpretive signs, perhaps buy a postcard to remember the vastness of a landscape normally viewed at a squint, too close to really understand.

When I travel I often send home postcards to myself, cryptic messages that urge me to remember my best self. These aren't missives meant for public consumption, carefully crafted and literary. No, I say stupid things like, "Remember this, floating in the warm waters of the Adriatic and being completely yourself," or "Remember that full moon? Remember that feeling of being at peace in the world?" Always these postcards—when they arrive in my mailbox after I've returned home—take me by surprise. Always I forget that I've written them, so that when a colorful, slick card falls out from among the bills and advertisements I get a momentary shock of recognition when I glimpse my own handwriting. I take the card inside before reading it, turn it over carefully, curious but a little afraid to see what I have to say to myself. Always, the message begins with "Remember."

Maybe that's what healing is: a kind of remembering. An ancient remembering that can't be done with our misfiring brains alone, our faulty intellects. No, there's something animal in it, insight that can't necessarily be translated into human words.

I think that's what Franz Marc's animals did for him: aroused the discerning part of his brain, nudged new circuits to fire, told him which details matter and which do not. He remembered the animal parts of himself, and these transformed on his canvas in the form of red horses, leaping cows, recumbent deer, and sleeping dogs. Sometimes the animals are dead, and sometimes they are bewitched. Oftentimes they are solitary, but sometimes they jostle against one another in a field. In one of his later works, *The Fate of the Animals*, Marc paints wild horses and deer in a furious composition—heads flung back, necks exposed, sharp planes of color jutting in every direction, animals accosted by light.

Three years after *The Fate of the Animals*, Marc died in a WWI battle at the age of thirty-six. In a last letter from the front he wrote that "nothing is more calming than the prospect of the peace of death . . . it leads us back into normal 'being.' The space between birth and death is an exception, in which there is much to fear and suffer. The only true, constant, philosophical comfort is the awareness that this exceptional condition will pass and that 'I-consciousness' which is always restless . . . will again sink back into its wonderful peace before birth. . . ."

Peace before birth: perhaps this is what I seek out in my white dog—that is what I read into the posture of her small but regal back.

I suppose I'll need to paint my own Dog at the Edge of the World, or put her together through mosaic, placing a broken bit of tile here, a fragment of blue glass there, her white back a crescent of an ancient teacup. I'd put in a bead of a black eye, positioned just so, to make that sidelong, beckoning gaze I remember so well. I'll work on the perspective, adjust as necessary, make her small enough to show the enormity of the landscape at her feet. But not too small. She is not overwhelmed; I have to remember this. She may not know where she's going, but she understands where she's been. It might take a long time, this dog at the edge of the world—there are so many details to get right, so many small and infinite gestures.

Bodyguard

More than thirty years ago I asked a friend if he felt, as I did, a guiding spirit in his life, some being—not a god exactly, but more of a friendly bodyguard who nudged you this way and that as you bumbled along your daily paths. We sat perched in a tree at the time, a suburban tree with low branches that begged to be climbed, and we looked through a curtain of leaves at the smoggy horizon. The San Gabriels might have been a blur in the distance. Surely cars sped by on the street below, and airplanes swooped in over the valley on their final approach to LAX. I was about to leave for a trip to Europe with two girls I hardly knew, and this boy and I had kissed once, a long kiss, the kind that makes you feel connected to something other than flesh. I knew we would write long letters to one another while I was gone, letters full of sighs and undefined longing. We sat in that tree together and swung our legs like children.

"Sure," he said. "There's gotta be something."

"Right," I said, "but what *is* that something, exactly?"

He took my hand and held the back of it against his smooth cheek. In my journal, in England, I wrote "I think love might protect me and keep me safe," while I thought of my friend in the tree, the way we held hands so tightly and grinned.

Now, years later, I live alone in an old house with two animals who wake at dawn and nudge my feet, ready for the day to begin. I get up and feed them before feeding myself, watch as they shake themselves and stretch and amble outside in a ritual they know by heart. And now I think of love not as a bodyguard exactly, but as a dog who knows where she's going, even when she has no idea where she's going; she simply trots down the trail ahead of you and looks over her shoulder, curious as to whether you'll follow.